T0276240

The 500 Hidden Secrets of

CHICAGO

INTRODUCTION

"For the masses who do the city's labor also keep the city's heart."
— Nelson Algren

The first thing visitors tend to notice about Chicago is its scale. Towering buildings nod to the fact that this is the city where the skyscraper was born. Vast warehouses left over from the post-fire building boom echo with possibility. Lake Michigan glints from the east like an ocean, its choppy waves tickling the Lakefront Trail.

Yes, Chicago is big. Yes, it's beautiful. But it doesn't rest on its laurels.

This book is an homage to a city that's powered equally by labor and love. Chicago is full of people that take pride in their city – and, in turn, keep its heart, as Nelson Algren so famously wrote. From the pitch-perfect Tom Collins cocktail at a modest neighborhood bar to a bank building archive devoted to the history of house music, Chicagoans preserve their passions rather than shout them from the top of the Sears Tower. (Never Willis Tower. Not if you're a local.)

Take the El to Pilsen and pinch bites of *carnitas* with a fresh tortilla. Bike the Bloomingdale Trail to Logan Square and look for 'The Tamale Guy'. Drive down Lake Shore Drive to the Near South Side and wander the blocks of Record Row – or head northeast a few blocks to the haunted Glessner House. These pages are merely a starting point: a collection of one local's discoveries gathered from a few decades of wandering. So, go see for yourself.

HOW TO
USE THIS BOOK

This guide lists 500 things you need to know about Chicago in
100 different categories. Most of these are places to visit, with practical
information to help you find your way. Others are bits of information
that help you get to know the city and its habitants. The aim of this guide
is to inspire, not to cover the city from A to Z.

The places listed in the guide are given an address, including the
neighborhood (for example Lakeview or Lincoln Park), and a number. The
neighborhood and number allow you to find the locations on the maps
at the beginning of the book: first look for the map of the corresponding
neighborhood, then look for the right number. A word of caution
however: these maps are not detailed enough to allow you to find specific
locations in the city. You can obtain an excellent map from any tourist
office or in most hotels. Or the addresses can be located on a smartphone.

Please also bear in mind that cities change all the time. The chef who hits
a high note one day may be uninspiring on the day you happen to visit.
The hotel ecstatically reviewed in this book might suddenly go downhill
under a new manager. The bar considered one of the best cocktail bars
might be empty on the night you visit. This is obviously a highly personal
selection. You might not always agree with it. If you want to leave
a comment, recommend a bar or reveal your favorite secret place,
please visit the website *the500hiddensecrets.com* – you'll also find free tips
and the latest news about the series there – or follow *@500hiddensecrets*
on Instagram or Facebook and leave a comment.

THE AUTHOR

Lauren Viera has called Chicago home for more than 20 years. After visiting on a whim during a college break, she was drawn to the city's thrilling music scene, fantastic Mexican food and friendly people, and fell for the historic architecture, cultural diversity and beautiful show of seasons.

While on staff at *Time Out Chicago* and the *Chicago Tribune*, and contributing to publications including *Chicago Magazine*, the *Chicago Reader* and *Crain's Chicago Business*, Lauren has been fortunate to dig deep into the city's culture from a reporter's point of view. With assignments ranging from the opening of the Art Institute's Modern Wing to discovering the loudest bands in the Ukrainian Village, she has grown to know and love the people, places and things that make Chicago so wonderfully unique.

Beyond writing, Lauren's passion for the city extends to teaching, gardening, preservation, volunteering, and advocating for representation from a diverse cross-section of residents. There are so many things she loves about Chicago, narrowing them down to 500 was a challenge.

The author wishes to thank all of the people who shared their secrets to grow and diversify the list of treasures that made it into the book. Special thanks to Sam Landers at Trope for the referral, Dettie Luyten at Luster for editing and advice, photographer Giovanni Simeone for lovingly capturing the city, and Rick Kogan for embodying Chicago through and through.

CHICAGO

community areas overview

Map 1–3 Central
Near North, The Loop, Near South

Map 4 West Side
Humboldt Park, West Town, West & East Garfield Park, Near West Side, North & South Lawndale, Lower West Side

Map 5 North Side
North Center, Lakeview, Avondale, Logan Square, Lincoln Park

Map 6 Northwest Side
Portage Park, Irving Park, Dunning, Montclare, Belmont Cragin, Hermosa

Map 6 Far North Side
O'Hare, Jefferson Park, Forest Glen, North Park, Albany Park, West Ridge, Lincoln Square, Rogers Park, Edgewater, Uptown

Map 7 South Side
Bridgeport, Armor Square, Douglas, Fuller Park, Grand Boulevard, Oakland, Kenwood, Washington Park, Hyde Park, Woodlawn, Greater Grand Crossing, South Shore

Southwest Side
Garfield Ridge, Archer Heights, Brighton Park, McKinley Park, West Elsdon, Gage Park, New City, West Lawn, Chicago Lawn, West Englewood, Englewood

Map 8 Far Southeast Side
Chatham, Avalon Park, South Chicago, Burnside, Calumet Heights, Roseland, Pullman, South Deering, East Side, West Pullman, Riverdale, Hegewisch

Far Southwest Side
Ashburn, Auburn Gresham, Beverly, Washington Heights, Mount Greenwood, Morgan Park

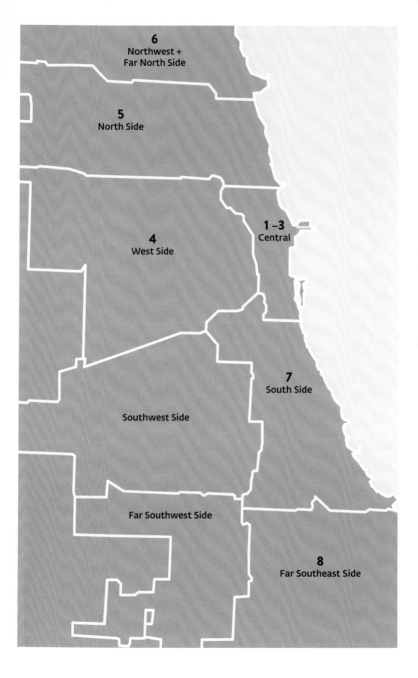

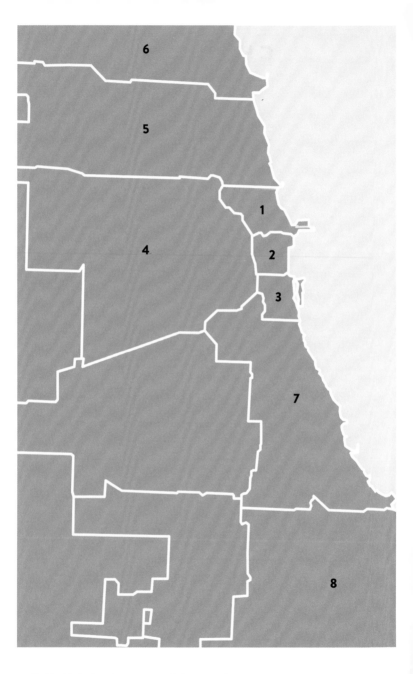

CHICAGO
neighborhoods overview

Map 1

CENTRAL—NEAR NORTH

Old Town, Gold Coast, Cabrini-Green, Magnificent Mile, River West, Fulton River District, River North, Streeterville, Navy Pier

Lake Michigan

Gold
Coast

Oak St
Beach

N Michigan Ave

S DuSable Lk Shr Dr

Magnificent
Mile

Milton Lee
Olive Park

E Ontario St

Ohio St
Beach

Streeterville

Navy Pier

Chicago River

E Wacker Dr

318
408
197
400
65
405
288
417
389
211
387
221 330
157
392
127
308
410
262
419 447
59 198 226
44
412
239
404

Map 2
CENTRAL—THE LOOP
Riverwalk, New East Side, Millennium Park, The Loop, Printers Row, South Loop

Map 3

CENTRAL–NEAR SOUTH

*Museum Campus, Chinatown, Prairie District,
Motor Row District*

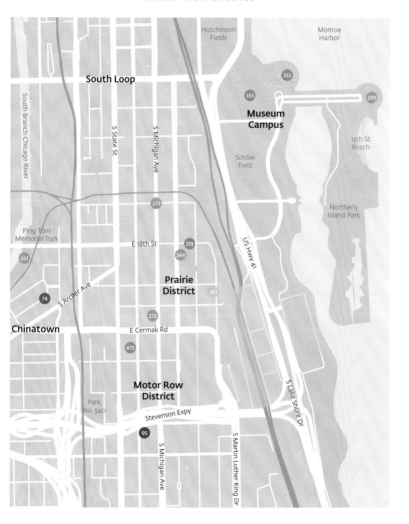

Map 4
WEST SIDE

Humboldt Park, West Town, Ukrainian Village, Wicker Park, East Village, Noble Square, Fulton Market, West Loop, West Loop Gate

EAT — **DRINK** — SHOP — BUILDINGS — DISCOVER — **CULTURE** — CHILDREN — SLEEP — **WEEKEND** — RANDOM

Wicker Park

294 295
12 158
287
378 106 93 459
51
269 86 136
Wicker 441
Park
185 144

Ashland Ave
Kennedy Expy

101
W Division St
21 464 182
141
Ukrainian
Village
247
East Noble
Village Square
Eckhart
174 85 Park
48 146 428
310 14 446
130 150 152 306 W Chicago Ave
177
West Town

N Damen Ave
149 13 41
168 309 W Grand Ave 27
N Ogden Ave

50 W Fulton St 176 40 62
123 46 120 376 406 55 124
Fulton Market 90
94 390 470
W Randolph St 341 380 100 21 49
382 29 37 307 61
W Madison St West Loop West Loop
Gate
Union 364
Park 215
Kennedy Expy

S Halsted St
Skinner 274 461
Park
W Adams St
64
W Jackson Blvd Chicago-Kansas City Expy

216 472

EAT — **DRINK** — SHOP — BUILDINGS — DISCOVER — **CULTURE** — CHILDREN — SLEEP — WEEKEND — RANDOM

Map 5

NORTH SIDE

Avondale, North Center, Lakeview, Logan Square, Bucktown,
West DePaul, Sheffield Neighbors, Lincoln Park, Ranch Triangle

EAT — **DRINK** — SHOP — BUILDINGS — DISCOVER — **CULTURE** — CHILDREN — SLEEP — WEEKEND — RANDOM

W Irving Park Rd

Lake Michigan

N Clark St

266

331

429

391

W Addison St

Ashland Ave

S Halsted St

S DuSable Lk Sh Dr

7

160

Belmont
Harbor

430

W Belmont Ave

Lakeview

437

N Lincoln Ave

268 45

112

415

W Diversy Pkwy

230

34

30

West DePaul

358

S DuSable Lk Sh Dr

217 471

N Clark St

333 69

W Fullerton Ave

99

241

453

2

442

360

72

Lincoln Park

Sheffield
Neighbors

Oz
Park

246

212 474

Lincoln
Park

43

28

283

W Armitage Ave

222

422

North Ave
Beach

166 363

Ranch Triangle

401

439

467

58

284

W North Ave

EAT — **DRINK** — SHOP — BUILDINGS — DISCOVER — **CULTURE** — CHILDREN — SLEEP — WEEKEND — RANDOM

Map 6
FAR NORTH SIDE
& NORTHWEST SIDE

O'Hare, Park Ridge, Niles, Forest Glen, North Park, West Ridge, Rogers Park, Edgewater, Andersonville, Kimball, Lincoln Square, Ravenswood, Uptown, Portage Park, Irving Park

Map 7

SOUTH SIDE

Bridgeport, Douglas, Bronzeville, Canaryville, Oakland, Kenwood, Hyde Park, Jackson Park, Englewood

EAT — **DRINK** — SHOP — BUILDINGS — DISCOVER — **CULTURE** — CHILDREN — SLEEP — WEEKEND — RANDOM

Map 8
FAR SOUTHEAST SIDE
Chatham, East Side, Pullman, South Deering

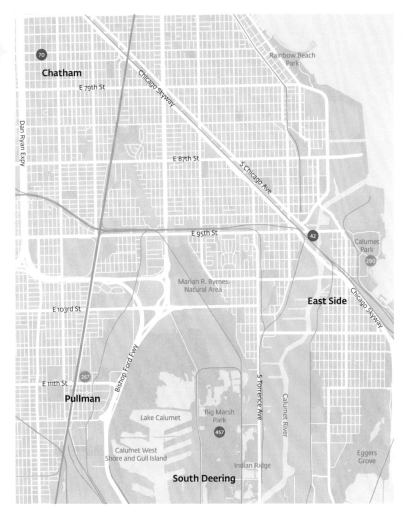

Chatham

Rainbow Beach Park

E 79th St

Chicago Skyway

E 87th St

S Chicago Ave

Dan Ryan Expy

E 95th St

Calumet Park

Marian R. Byrnes
Natural Area

Chicago Skyway

E 103rd St

East Side

Bishop Ford Fwy

E 111th St

Pullman

Lake Calumet

Big Marsh Park

S Torrence Ave

Calumet River

Calumet West
Shore and Gull Island

Indian Ridge

Eggers Grove

South Deering

PORTO

80 PLACES
TO EAT OR BUY
GOOD FOOD

5 styles of **PIZZA**

---

1 **NEW YORK STYLE**
AT: DANTE'S
3028 W Armitage
Avenue
Logan Square ⑤
+1 773 342 0002
danteschicago.com

Dante's only serves one size of pizza: enormous. Famous for its pitch-perfect take on floppy, greasy, extra-large New York-style slices, the mini-chain serves wood-fired pizzas primarily destined for delivery to the North Side, as well as to-go and dine-in slices from its Ukrainian Village and Logan Square locations.

2 **DEEP DISH**
AT: PEQUOD'S PIZZA
2207 N Clybourn
Avenue
Sheffield Neighbors ⑤
+1 773 327 1512
pequodspizza.com

Caramelized crust. This is the legacy of Pequod's Pizza, arguably Chicago's most beloved pizza institution. Born in a northwest suburb in 1970, Pequod's serves deep dish and thin-crust pies that respectfully trump the city's braggart megachains (Giordano's and Lou Malnati's) in spite of its laissez-faire approach.

3 **DETROIT STYLE**
AT: PAULIE GEE'S
2451 N Milwaukee
Avenue
Logan Square ⑤
+1 773 360 1072
pauliegee.com/
logan-square

Paulie Gee is a Brooklyn-based pizza fanatic who has since franchised a half-dozen shops around the country, but the Logan Square outpost is best known for a totally different take: Detroit-style pizza. Flash-fired in a deep, square dish with extra crispy toppings, the 'Hellboy' with soppressata and 'Mike's Hot Honey' are must-tries.

4 NEAPOLITAN STYLE

AT: SPACCA NAPOLI

1769 W Sunnyside
Avenue
Ravenswood ⑥
+1 773 878 2420
spaccanapoli
pizzeria.com

Perched on a sunny corner with a crowd of first-dates, families, and everyone in between spilling onto its patio, Spacca Napoli is an authentic homage to rustic, Neapolitan-style pizza. Chewy crust, just-burst tomatoes, and mozzarella cheese are spread in a symphony, sprinkled with fresh basil and accompanied by juicy wines. It's enough to make you say *mangia.*

5 TAVERN STYLE

AT: VITO & NICK'S

8433 S Pulaski Road
Ashburn
+1 773 735 2050
vitoandnicks.com

Locals have long regarded this South Side original as one of the best spots in the city for authentic tavern-style pizza. Serving pizza since the 1940s, Vito & Nick's specializes in cracker-thin crust loaded heavy with tangy sauce, traditional toppings, and a thick coating of bubbly cheese, best washed down with a pitcher of Old Style.

3 PAULIE GEE'S

6 **LULA CAFE**

5 NEIGHBORHOOD *go-tos*

6 **LULA CAFE**
2537 N Kedzie Boulevard
Logan Square [5]
+1 773 489 9554
lulacafe.com

The city's (and perhaps the country's) original farm-to-table restaurant, Lula opened in 1999 and, miraculously, has seldom repeated a specials menu since. From unique brunch dishes to lush, coursed-out dinners featuring farm-fresh produce and protein, it's a favorite destination for locals as well as visitors in-the-know. Don't skip dessert: the carrot cake is a must.

7 **SOUTHPORT GROCERY AND CAFE**
3552 N Southport
Lakeview [5]
+1 773 665 0100
southportgrocery.com

With just enough tables to accommodate popping in for breakfast or lunch (and secret dinners), this bustling staple in the heart of Lincoln Park's shopping district prides itself on from-scratch favorites like quiches with fresh ingredients, finger-lickin' sweet entrees, and chopped salads that rotate with the seasons. The grocery features housemade preserves and local purveyors.

8 KIMSKI

954–960 W 31st St
Bridgeport ⑦
+1 773 823 7336

Borne of its owner (and unofficial mayor of Bridgeport) Ed Marszewski's Korean and Polish heritage, Kimski features signature flavors from each cuisine in delightfully unique dishes. Try the veggie *potskis* filled with sauerkraut and mushroom, herb salad and pickled onion; or the sweet-and-spicy 'Ko-Po' wings. Dishes are relatively small and affordable, perfect for sharing.

9 MEDICI ON 57TH

1327 E 57th St
Hyde Park ⑦
+1 773 667 7394
medici57.com

A comforting all-day restaurant in the heart of University of Chicago's retail district, Medici on 57th has been feeding town and gown alike since the early 1960s. Serving coffee all day (and into the night), pizzas, burgers, hearty soups, several salads, and an array of fried finger-food staples, Medici has something for everyone.

10 MANNY'S CAFETERIA & DELI

1141 S Jefferson St
South Loop ②
+1 312 939 2855
mannysdeli.com

No frills, 80-year-old institution serving all-day staples. Established as a working-class cafeteria doling out generous portions of Jewish cooking, Manny's offers lunchroom classics: corned beef sandwiches, liver & onions, meatloaf, matzo ball soup, and more. A favorite of local politicians and lawmakers, it's still a go-to lunch spot for former president Barack Obama.

5 of the very best
BAKERIES

11 **SUGAR MOON**
3612 W Wrightwood Avenue
Logan Square ⑤
sugarmoonchicago.com

There's a long queue on most mornings, and for good reason. From crusty, savory tarts to its famous tahini chocolate chip cookies and tiramisu-flavored Cloud Cookies, Sugar Moon has earned fans since it opened in 2021. Grab a coffee down the street at Necessary & Sufficient Coffee for the wait.

11 SUGAR MOON

12 MINDY'S BAKERY

1623 N Milwaukee
Avenue
Wicker Park ④
+1 773 489 1747
mindysbakery.com

To say Mindy Segal is an accomplished baker is an understatement. At her former restaurant, HotChocolate, she won a James Beard Award for Outstanding Pastry Chef and a cult following for her rich hot chocolates and housemade marshmallows. Go for indulgent takes on French classics and some of the city's best bagels.

13 AYA PASTRY

1332 W Grand
Avenue
West Town ④
+1 312 846 6186
ayapastry.com

Can a banana bread loaf change your life? This is the power of Aya Fukai's handiwork. The Michelin-starred, James Beard-nominated pastry chef initially opened her bakery as a wholesale supplier for local restaurants. Five years later, Aya Pastry has expanded her business to meet demands of her citywide sweet-tooth fans.

14 WEST TOWN BAKERY

1916 W Chicago
Avenue
West Town ④
+1 773 904 1414
westtownbakery.com

Heavier bakes, notably anything cake-related, are this classic bakery's calling cards. Decadent, moist cupcakes, bite-size cake balls, and unique signature cakes can all be made vegan, gluten-free, or meet other dietary restrictions, and taste just as delicious if not more so. Outposts are scattered throughout the city.

15 ROESER'S BAKERY

3216 W North
Avenue
Humboldt Park ④
+1 773 489 6900
roeserscakes.com

The antithesis of a trendy bake shop, Roeser's has been perfecting its recipes since 1911, making it the oldest family-owned bakery in Chicago. The shop opened with Scandinavian staples like strudel and rye bread but today, its cases are some of the most diverse in town.

5 **MEXICAN** *musts*

16 **MI TOCAYA ANTOJERIA**
2800 W Logan Boulevard
Logan Square [5]
+1 872 315 3947
mitocaya.com

Chef Diana Dávila's "namesake" pays tribute to her Mexican heritage, serving some of the very best food in the city. Tucked onto a charming residential corner of Logan Square, the restaurant's unapologetic celebration of flavors and ingredients paired with passionate service keep patrons coming back to enjoy menus inspired by each season.

17 **L'PATRON**
3749 W Fullerton Avenue
Logan Square [5]
+1 773 252 6335
lpatrontacos.com

There is no shortage of delicious tacos in Chicago. But since opening on a busy parkway in 2012, L'Patron has been the North Side spot to beat. Popular standards include *al pastor* and *pollo adobado*, but don't miss L'Patron's take on the *pescado*: beer-battered tilapia served with a tangy serrano aioli dressed cabbage.

18 **CARNITAS URUAPAN**
1725 West 18th St
Pilsen
+1 312 226 2654
carnitasurua panchi.com

Chicagoans have a love affair with *carnitas* ('little meats') – pulled pork stewed to perfection – and at Carnitas Uruapan's duo of busy restaurants, *carnitas* are the main event. Order a half-pound served simply with corn tortillas, or as a dinner plate with homestyle-refried beans, a crispy taco and pork skin *chicharrones*.

19 KIE-GOL-LANEE

5004 N Sheridan
Road
Uptown ⑥
+1 872 241 9088
kiegol.com

The warm ambiance of this storefront Oaxacan restaurant comes alive the instant the gracious staff gets you settled with a bowl of chips and a dish of red mole sauce. From simply delicious tacos and tostadas to meaty mains like stewed rabbit, grilled quail and roasted cornish hen, everything is worth trying – even the authentic *chapulines*.

20 5 RABANITOS

1758 West 18th St
Pilsen
+1 312 285 2710
5rabanitos.com

Lively music and a busy, energetic staff keep customers happy at this modest Mexican spot. Expert interpretations of regional favorites like *cochinita pibil* live alongside originals like grilled chicken with garlic-honey marinade, and the tortas are so big, they can stand on one end.

16 MI TOCAYA ANTOJERIA

5 *great* DATE SPOTS

21 AVEC

615 W Randolph St
West Loop Gate ④
+1 312 377 2002
avecrestaurant.com

Jovial staff, a killer wine list, and a warm and intimate dining room make Avec feel special from the moment you walk in. Start with the chorizo-stuffed Medjool date – a menu staple since 2017 – and ease into the 'Mediterranean meets Midwest' menu, a handful of shared plates at a time.

22 LE BOUCHON

1958 N Damen
Avenue
Bucktown ⑤
+1 773 862 6600
*lebouchon
ofchicago.com*

There's a reason this tiny French bistro has been packed every night for the past 25 years: it's a classic. Serving Parisian staples like caramelized onion soup with gruyere, escargots in garlic and parsley butter, and a hearty cassoulet, it's a no-brainer for first dates – or 50th.

23 GIANT

3209 W Armitage
Avenue
Logan Square ⑤
+1 773 252 0997
giantrestaurant.com

The room is small, but Giant's flavors are big. Decadent housemade pasta dishes are the star: get the bucatini with bacon, jalapeño and anchovy; or the saffron tagliatelle with Dungeness crab and chilli butter; or both, with expertly prepared veg, perfect little corn biscuits, great cocktails, and a refreshing wine list. Every single thing is good.

24 THE ITALIAN VILLAGE

71 W Monroe St
The Loop ②
+1 312 332 7005
*italianvillage-
chicago.com*

Tuxedoed waiters. White tablecloths. Red sauce. The city's oldest Italian restaurant hasn't changed much since opening in 1927. Of the three dining rooms, The Village is the one to book, with whimsical seating areas like a confession booth. Don't miss the wine list: 1300 varietals strong, it's the largest collection in the Midwest.

25 VIRTUE

1462 East 53rd St
Hyde Park ⑦
+1 773 947 8831
virtuerestaurant.com

Serving devilishly delicious Southern comfort food paired with wine and cocktails, Virtue threatens to monopolize the dinner conversation – it's that good. Biscuits with pimento cheese, gulf shrimp and green tomatoes with traditional remoulade sauce, blackened catfish – it's all here, plus bread pudding for dessert. Impress your date by ordering enough for leftovers.

5 **ROMANTIC** *dinners*

26 BISTRO CAMPAGNE

4518 N Lincoln Avenue
Lincoln Square [6]
+1 773 271 6100
bistrocampagne.com

Step past the dainty little bar at this quaint and charming French bistro, and a series of cozy rooms unfold one after the other, giving way to candlelit tables that invite lingering over bites of brandade and pain perdu. In warmer months, a lush courtyard adds to the ambiance.

27 LA SCAROLA

721 W Grand Avenue
West Town [4]
+1 312 243 1740
lascarola.com

Tucked into a small storefront on a busy crossroad, this sweet little Italian spot is known for its photograph-covered walls, intimately spaced tables and familial staff. Serving hearty portions of comfort food like crispy bruschetta, breaded calamari and sumptuous eggplant parmesan, it's been a romantic classic since 1998.

28 GEJA'S CAFE

340 W Armitage Avenue
Old Town [5]
+1 773 281 9101
gejascafe.com

Housed in a candlelit, wine cellar-like room with live flamenco music and a menu full of fondue for two, it's no wonder Geja's is widely recognized as one of the most romantic restaurants in the city. Take turns dipping protein, veg and breads, and the house Belgian chocolate fondue for dessert.

29 THE PRESS ROOM

1134 W Washington Boulevard
West Loop ④
+1 312 450 3301
pressroomchicago.com

The hauntingly romantic aura of this subterranean wine-driven spot could be due to its history. Once upon a time, the 1909 building housed a casket factory. These days, the only spirits you'll encounter are in the expertly poured cocktails, served with small bites and shareable mains. Need a room? The owners run a B&B upstairs.

30 NORTH POND

2610 N Cannon Drive
Lincoln Park ⑤
+1 773 477 5845
northpond restaurant.com

This exquisite fine dining restaurant in lovely Lincoln Park is accessible via a serene walking path. It's housed in a 1912 ice skating warming shelter pristinely restored in the arts and crafts style. Views of the surrounding park are stunning year round, and both brunch and dinner experiences are built around tasting menus.

30 NORTH POND

5 takes on the
CHICAGO HOT DOG

---

31 **SUPERDAWG**

**6363 N Milwaukee
Avenue
Norwood Park East** ⑥
+1 773 763 0660
superdawg.com

One of the oldest operating car-hops in the country. All-beef dogs are made to order with co-owner Maurie Berman's 'symphony of colors': golden mustard, neon green piccalilli relish, white onions, green pickled tomato, sport peppers, and a kosher dill pickle with celery salt, served on a bed of crinkle-cut fries. "Ketchup," Berman said, "would be an abomination."

32 **FIXIN' FRANKS**

AT: THE HOME DEPOT
**2570 N Elston
Avenue
Bucktown** ⑤
+1 773 289 4615

Operating tiny stands within a corporate home building supply chain, Fixin' Franks serves a half-dozen different sausage-and-bun combos, from Polish sausage to Italian beef topped with local favorite J.P. Graziano giardiniera. For a few dollars more (and a bit longer wait), the Wagyu beef hot dog – with everything, of course – is the way to go.

33 VIENNA BEEF FACTORY STORE

3847 S Morgan Avenue
Bridgeport ⑦
+1 773 435 2298
viennabeef.com

This is the one that started it all, thanks to a Viennese hot-dog stand set up just outside the Chicago World's Fair of 1893. Vienna Beef is still the sausage king of Chicago, and you can't get any closer to the real deal than a dog from this cheery yellow-roofed counter-service spot across from the factory.

34 THE WIENERS CIRCLE

2622 N Clark St
Lincoln Park West ⑤
+1 773 477 7444
wienerscircle chicago.com

Flame-charred dogs and fresh attitudes are served until the wee hours. Since opening 40 years ago, it's been a divisive destination for locals and tourists alike, as customers are often grilled as severely as the meat. Still, the Vienna Red Hot Charror Steam is spot-on, the fries are particularly delicious, and the politics lean correct.

35 JIMMY'S RED HOTS

4000 W Grand Avenue
Humboldt Park ④
+1 773 384 9513
jimmysredhots chicago.com

Step inside this odd little brick building and you're instantly transported back to the 1950s, when Jimmy Faruggia started selling Depression-style hot dogs topped with mustard, relish, onion, and sport peppers. The place is so averse to ketchup, it's written on the workers' shirts alongside a ketchup bottle with a slash through it: "No Ketchup Never Ever."

5 STEAKHOUSES

36 GENE & GEORGETTI

500 N Franklin St
River North ①
+1 312 527 3718
geneandgeorgetti.com

Founded in 1941, the city's oldest steakhouse is the epitome of a classic. A maze of dining rooms and additions mark the original location on a bustling corner of River North, where dry martinis, shrimp cocktails, and a half-dozen 21-day wet-aged steaks and chops are served to a colorful crowd of locals and tourists alike.

37 EL CHE STEAKHOUSE & BAR

845 W Washington
Boulevard
West Loop ④
+1 312 265 1130
elchechicago.com

Housed in the beautifully renovated former Checker Taxi building, El Che is a vibrant, vivacious tribute to South American wood-fired cooking. All of the cuts here are served with mouthwatering chimichurri sauce, and the range of grilled seafood – from diavola-buttered lobster tail to lime-aioli head-on shrimp – shouldn't be missed.

38 BAVETTE'S BAR & BOEUF

218 W Kinzie St
River North ①
+1 312 624 8154
bavettessteakhouse.com

Rich leather booths, vintage chandeliers, and gilded mirrors elevate this stylish French-accented steakhouse into date-night territory. From its oversized wedge salad to its indulgent hot fudge sundae, the details beyond the beef are what make Bavette's truly special. Don't miss the cocktails: the cognac Sazerac complements the filet mignon like they're going steady.

39 GIBSON'S ITALIA

233 N Canal St
Fulton River
District ①
+1 312 414 1100
gibsonsitalia.com

Though technically not a steakhouse, Gibson's Italia shares its name – and its grass-fed Australian cuts – with its sister steakhouse in the Gold Coast. Prime Angus and Carrara Wagyu are also on offer, as is a full menu of Italian staples. And unlike its sister location, Gibson's Italia has one of the best views of the Chicago River.

40 SWIFT & SONS

1000 W Fulton
Market
Fulton Market ④
+1 312 733 9420
swiftandsons chicago.com

A handsome nod to the traditional steakhouses of the early 20th century, Swift & Sons features a beautifully wood-paneled dining room accented with curves and warm lighting to complement a decadent menu of steakhouse standards. Fans of the raw bar and lighter fare should check out Cold Storage: a sister restaurant that specializes in fish and seafood.

5 **SEAFOOD** *spots*

---

41 **BIG STAR MARISCOS**

551 N Ogden Avenue
West Town ④
+1 312 521 5169
bigstarmariscos.com

The seafood sister to the popular Big Star taco restaurants, Mariscos marries a fun and festive atmosphere with a modest menu full of ceviches, *cócteles*, and a half-dozen tacos and tostadas, including a few standard meat-based versions. Service is friendly, food comes out fast, the drinks are strong, and in warm weather months, the patio is poppin'.

42 **CALUMET FISHERIES**

3259 E 95th St
East Side ⑧
+1 773 933 9855
calumetfisheries.com

A rock's throw from the Indiana state line, this 1940s fish shack draws locals for its venerable spread of smoked fish, fried shrimp, crab cakes and more. There's no seating, so customers have taken to eating Calumet's dinners (fish, fries, coleslaw and sauce) right in their cars parked in front of the building.

43 **DIRK'S FISH & GOURMET SHOP**

2070 N Clybourn Avenue
Sheffield Neighbors 5
+1 773 404 3475
dirksfish.com

There's not much ambiance at this stripmall fishmonger's shop where locals pick up fresh fish for dinner. But the handful of tables are often full: Dirk has the hookup to some of the freshest fish in the city and offers a full menu, from lobster rolls to sushi. On Saturdays, he's out front grilling whatever's fresh.

44 **SHAW'S CRAB HOUSE**

21 E Hubbard St
River North 1
+1 312 527 2722
shawscrabhouse.com

Doing double-duty as a formal white-tableclothed restaurant and a lively traditional raw bar with a black-and-white chequered floor, Shaw's is a local favorite for traditional seafood. Oysters and crab cakes are a must, but from there, anything goes. There's as much sushi on the menu as fresh fish entrees, plus surf & turf options.

45 **FISH BAR**

2956 N Sheffield Avenue
Lakeview 5
+1 773 687 8026
3rdcoastfishbar.com

The small menu and casual atmosphere make Fish Bar easy for a low-key meal. But with a decorated chef behind the concept, the food hits above and beyond expectations. There are plenty of delicious main dishes to choose from, but the go-to is the hearty lobster roll – one of the city's best.

5 SPLURGE-WORTHY
dinners

---

46 NEXT

953 W Fulton Market
Fulton Market ④
nextrestaurant.com

If you can't get into Alinea, the city's only three-starred Michelin restaurant, you might get lucky with Next, Chef Grant Achatz's extravagant, thematic fine dining experience. Past menus have paid tribute to everything from 'childhood' to Tokyo to the World's Fair, and even Alinea itself. Dinners are ticketed based on day and time and priced accordingly.

47 RPM ITALIAN

52 W Illinois St
River North ①
+1 312 222 1888
rpmrestaurants.com

Of the trio of RPM restaurants in town, RPM Italian shines the brightest. Why? The pasta. Yes, the vast dining room is sexy and sleek. Yes, the service is impeccable. But the short rib bolognese; the duck, pork ragu and smoked ricotta rigatoni; the bucatini with fresh pomodoro tomatoes and Genovese basil – these are memorable meals.

48   PORTO

**1600 W Chicago
Avenue
West Town** ④
+1 312 600 6336
portochicago.com

Rare is the restaurant whose interior design is as gorgeous as the food. At Porto, an homage to Spanish and Portuguese seaside cuisine starts with the library of tin fish displayed atop the bar, and ends with devastatingly delicious creations like Jamón Ibérico ice cream. Everything is coursed out beautifully, so plan to stay awhile.

49   SEPIA

**123 N Jefferson St
West Loop Gate** ④
+1 312 441 1920
sepiachicago.com

Housed in a former print shop building from the 1890s, the dining room nods to the restaurant's namesake with plush neutrals, warm woods, and crystal details that light up the room. Classic American dishes are expertly prepared with modern flair, and the house cocktails, which are as seasonally inclined as the menu, are a must.

50   EVER

**1340 W Fulton St
Fulton Market** ④
ever-restaurant.com

Star chef Curtis Duffy's fine dining restaurant offers exclusively tasting menus – eight or ten courses – pulling from the fresh seasonality of the Midwest, parsed out into two-hour experiences. Here, the presentation is on as high a plane as the ingredients themselves. Following dinner, book a round of cocktails and digestifs at After, the chef's upscale spirits lounge.

5 LATE-NIGHT *bites*

---

51 BIG STAR

**1531 N Damen
Avenue
Wicker Park** ④
+1 773 235 4039
bigstarchicago.com

A classic since 2009. The hours-long waits have waned, but it remains a go-to for all-day and late-night tacos, tequila and bourbon. If you're on the go, head to the take-out window for a walking taco: spicy bean dip, cholula salsa, chihuahua cheese, onion, cilantro and a dollop of crema piled into a bag of Fritos.

51 BIG STAR

52 ARTURO'S TACOS

2001 N Western Avenue
Bucktown (5)
+1 773 772 4944
arturos-tacos.com

For decades, two neighboring taco joints have tempted late-night crowds with complimentary chips and salsa, nearly identical taco menus, and competitive pricing. The only real difference is the ambiance: Arturo's has a cozy diner feel with just enough booths, and remains open until the wee hours: 5 am on the weekends, and 2 am through the week.

53 *TAMALES* FROM 'THE TAMALE GUY'

AT: QUALITY TIME
2934 W Diversey Avenue
Avondale (5)
qualitytimebar.com

In the early aughts, 'The Tamale Guy' (aka Claudio Velez) pedalled fresh and filling *tamales* from a cooler to late-night bars on the North Side. These days, Velez is settled at Quality Time, a delightfully low-key cocktail bar, where his cheese, chicken and pork *tamales* are on the permanent menu.

54 SKYLARK

2149 S Halsted St
Pilsen
+1 312 624 8583
skylarkchicago.com

A lack of pretence lends this divey bar a ton of street cred. Beyond the microbrews on tap, there's premium pub fare, from the deliciously juicy Skylark Burger topped with coleslaw and onion rings, to a grilled salmon sandwich served with a schmear of lemon horseradish aioli and mixed greens on an Italian roll.

55 SUNNYGUN

664 W Lake St
West Loop (4)
+1 312 600 0600
sunnygunchicago.com

Sunnygun, sharing its kitchen with sister bar Moneygun, serves late-night bites and solid cocktails. The cheery patio's picnic tables and bocce ball court create a casual feel, while the rolling El tracks overhead justify the loud music and conversation.

5 **HIDDEN** *restaurants*

56 **OASIS CAFE**
21 N Wabash Avenue
The Loop ②
+1 312 443 9534
*oasiscafeon
wabash.com*

The definition of a hidden gem, this traditional Middle Eastern and Mediterranean spot is tucked into the rear of a jewelry store within the Wabash Jewelry Mall. Follow the signs and your nose to a full menu featuring an eclectic offering of Moroccan-style lamb kebab, spinach pie, grape leaves, creamy hummus, falafel and more.

57 **A TAVOLA**
2148 W Chicago Avenue
Ukrainian Village ④
+1 773 276 7567
atavolachi.com

Located in an unassuming brick home that's covered with ivy most of the year, A Tavola has been hiding in plain sight since 1995, churning out delicious Northern Italian comfort food. Located within the ground floor parlor, the space is quiet and intimate, filled with the aromas of expertly made gnocchi, juicy Sangiovese, and succulent roast chicken.

58 **ADA STREET**

1664 N Ada St
Clybourn Corridor [5]
+1 773 234 1753
adastreetchicago.com

When this new American eatery opened on a dark industrial corridor off Goose Island, there was virtually no signage, leaving first-time visitors to wonder whether they were in the wrong place. It's now clearly marked but fortunately has maintained its hushed charm. Great food, great wines and an all-vinyl soundtrack keep locals coming back for more.

59 **BILLY GOAT TAVERN**

430 N Michigan Avenue
Magnificent Mile [1]
+1 312 222 1525
billygoattavern.com

Despite its fame, the original Billy Goat is not easy to find. Follow the signs from Upper Michigan Avenue down the stairs, and you'll eventually be greeted by the tiny diner's colorful signage paying homage to 90 years of cheeseburgers – and the infamous curse of The Billy Goat.

60 **EL IDEAS**

2419 West 14th St
Douglass Park
+1 312 226 8144
elideas.com

In a free-standing building on an anonymous West Side cul-de-sac, this test kitchen–turned–upscale restaurant breaks all the rules of fine dining. In a kitchen larger than the dining space, chef Philip Foss and his staff steer the evening's tasting menu, plating coursed dinners to intimate weekend crowds. The 'EL' is short for 'elevated'.

5 FOOD HALLS
and MARKETS

---

61 CHICAGO FRENCH MARKET
131 N Clinton St
West Loop Gate ④
+1 312 575 0306
frenchmarket chicago.com

Modest food court anchored by European vendors. Near the center of the hub wafts a constant aroma of fresh crepes. Just behind it are standard Italian paninis and antipasti salads. Other vendors run the gamut from Chinese street food to Australian-style hand pies to a traditional Dutch *frietkot* (fry shack).

62 TIME OUT MARKET
916 W Fulton Market
Fulton Market ④
+1 312 637 3888
timeoutmarket.com

Trendy food court featuring satellite locations of beloved local spots. Grab soup and dumplings from Urbanbelly, the Korean small-bites spot with a French accent, or head straight to its sister spot, Bill Kim Ramen Bar. The simply named Bar features cocktails from mixologists and microbrewers all over town.

63 REVIVAL FOOD HALL
125 S Clark St
The Loop ②
+1 773 999 9411
revivalfoodhall.com

Housed in the beautifully restored National building in the heart of the Loop. Take your tray of Indian street food, fresh poke, or German-inspired comfort grub and find a spot at the library table near Curbside Books & Records, where you can browse vinyl from local bands.

64 FROM HERE ON

433 W Van Buren St
West Loop Gate ④
fromhereonchicago.com

This hip, airy food hall is tucked into the ground floor of the massive Old Post Office: a 2,6-million-square-foot art deco building that recently reopened after an 800-million-dollar renovation. Don't miss the outdoor seating area, where views of the Loop skyline can be admired from a built-in hammock.

65 ASTER HALL

900 N Michigan
Avenue
Magnificent Mile ①
+1 312 720 2919
asterhallchicago.com

Located in one of the Mag Mile's most popular shopping complexes, Aster Hall is about as far from a mall food court as it gets. Under the direction of one of the city's most popular restaurateurs, this bi-level culinary hub features a cross-section of cuisine including a tiny outpost of the popular Small Cheval burger destination.

65 ASTER HALL

5 VEGETARIAN *spots*

66 **THE CHICAGO DINER**
2333 N Milwaukee Avenue
Logan Square [5]
+1 773 252 3211
veggiediner.com

"Meat-free since '83," this is the city's original vegetarian restaurant. It's since perfected its meat-free comfort food menu to draw vegetarians and omnivores alike. Spinach dip and Caesar salad live alongside seitan versions of standards like country fried steak, chili, and a BLT burger.

66 THE CHICAGO DINER

67 HANDLEBAR

2311 W North Avenue
Wicker Park [4]
+1 773 384 9546
handlebarchicago.com

This biker-friendly pub has been catering to the city's hipster community since it opened in 2003. Try the famous Green Meanie with avocado, herbed goat cheese, spinach, tomato and agave mustard served on perfectly toasted multigrain bread, or go for a meat-free 'chicken' wrap.

68 KALE MY NAME

3300 W Montrose Avenue
Kimball [6]
+1 872 208 7125
kalemyname.com

A delightfully bright all-day spot with an especially popular brunch menu, Kale My Name prides itself on vegan and gluten-free takes on classics like pancakes and Beyond Meat sausages, a filling breakfast burrito, and more. Be sure to add a side of rosemary potatoes to round out your plate.

69 FANCY PLANTS KITCHEN

1433 W Fullerton Avenue
West DePaul [5]
+1 773 857 0486
fancyplantskitchen.com

Founded by a past winner of *Vegan Iron Chef*, Fancy Plants Café and Fancy Plants Kitchen feature delicious, elevated vegan takes on standard fare. Utilizing the best ingredients and vegetables from the surrounding farm communities, as well as fermentation and preservation of ingredients, the Kitchen serves beautifully presented dishes in a five-course menu experience.

70 SOUL VEG CITY

203 E 75th St
Chatham [8]
+1 773 224 0104
soulvegcity.com

After four decades as a vegetarian destination, this plant-based mecca celebrated a grand re-opening in 2021. The menu still features the original restaurant's penchant for Southern-accented vegetarian food: jerk BBQ seitan, kale greens, juicy seitan sloppy joes, and more.

5 *spots for*
SWEET TREATS

71 **SAME DAY CAFE**
2651 N Kedzie Avenue
Logan Square [5]
+1 773 342 7040
samedaycafe.com

This all-day cafe is humble about its sweeter side, but it's so good. Flavorful syrups made in-house mean you can order a Chocolate, Wild Cherry, or Lemon Lavender Phosphate with your brunch, or skip straight to dessert with homemade ice creams, egg creams, and a half-dozen freshly baked cookies. The candied ginger molasses? Chef's kiss.

72 **SWEET MANDY B'S**
1208 W Webster Avenue
Sheffield Neighbors [5]
+1 773 244 1174
sweetmandybs.com

Sometimes, all you need is a really, really good cupcake. Sweet Mandy B's has been perfecting its cupcakes for more than 20 years, methodically topping them with a dreamy dollop of frosting presented just so. Perfectly symmetrical bars and cookies fill out the cases.

73 **BANG BANG PIE & BISCUITS**
2051 N California Avenue
Logan Square [5]
+1 773 276 8888
bangbangpie.com

Pie doesn't seem like a destination treat...until you've tried Bang Bang. This unintentionally pie-shaped storefront lures customers to its wonderfully aromatic space with its perfectly thick, brown, flaky crusts filled with delicious ingredients.

74 AJI ICHIBAN

2117 S China Place
Chinatown ③
+1 312 804 8686

Grab a basket as soon as you walk through the door of this Chinatown candy shop neatly arranged with bin after bin of colorful candy. Hard and soft, ginger and sour, chewy and crunchy – they're all on display and beg to be scooped by the pound. On the shelves are an assortment of hard-to-find packaged cookies and candy bars.

75 SPINNING J

1000 N California
Avenue
West Town ④
+1 872 829 2793
spinningj.com

Situated in a cute corner storefront dating to the 1930s, this throwback soda fountain and bake shop is a delightful destination. Every single detail is handled with care – from design choices like the hand-stenciled walls and vintage light fixtures, to the thick and crispy knuckle-pressed crust on the Key Lime Hibiscus Pie.

73 BANG BANG PIE & BISCUITS

5 *favorite*
ICE-CREAM *spots*

76 **PRETTY COOL ICE CREAM**
2353 N California Avenue
Logan Square ⑤
+1 773 697 4140
prettycoollogansquare.com

Covered in pink paint with stadium seating, Pretty Cool serves wow-worthy ice-cream popsicles. Unique flavors like Caramel Horchata Crunch, Mango Lassi, and Grasshopper are offered alongside creative interpretations of the basics. There are even plant pops for sweet-toothed vegans.

76 PRETTY COOL ICE CREAM

77 MARGIE'S CANDIES

1960 N Western Avenue
Bucktown [5]
+1 773 384 1035

One of the oldest ice-cream parlors in the city, Margie's looks the part. Locals love the ridiculously large sundaes and banana splits served traditionally with a swirl of whipped cream, Maraschino cherries on top, and wafer cookies on the side. Tableside jukeboxes, antique Tiffany lamps, and real milkshakes (with sidecars) complete the retro appeal.

78 THE ORIGINAL RAINBOW CONE

9233 S Western Avenue
Beverly
+1 773 238 9833
rainbowcone.com

This nearly century-old, cotton-candy pink ice-cream shop's signature menu item is a stack of five flavors – orange sherbet, pistachio, Palmer House (vanilla, cherries and walnuts, named after the famous hotel), strawberry, chocolate – sliced, not scooped, onto a very brave sugar cone.

79 THE FREEZE

2815 W Armitage Avenue
Logan Square [5]
+1 773 384 5211
facebook.com/thefreezechicago

This no-nonsense walk-up burgers and ice-cream shack has been a neighborhood go-to since it opened in 1950. Specialty sundaes and soft-serve cones are the most popular items; Bostons (half-shake, half-sundae) and Freezees (milkshake with added ingredients) round out the menu.

80 SCOOTER'S FROZEN CUSTARD

1658 W Belmont Avenue
West Lakeview [5]
+1 773 244 6415
scootersfrozencustard.com

Frozen custard is a Midwestern tradition, and no one in the city does it better than Scooter's. Vanilla and chocolate are daily standards, and thereafter, from-scratch flavors – chocolate cake batter, Snickers, cookies & cream – appear on a carefully updated 'schedule'.

THE BERGHOFF

55 PLACES FOR A DRINK

---

5 taverns that
SURVIVED
PROHIBITION

---

81 **THE BERGHOFF**
   17 W Adams St
   The Loop ②
   +1 312 427 7399
   theberghoff.com

This beloved bar's storied history dates back to the Chicago World's Fair of 1893, where a German immigrant named Herman Berghoff set up a roadside stand to sell his beers to fair-goers. Berghoff eventually opened a brick-and-mortar tavern, operated by the same German family ever since. During Prohibition, the place stayed afloat by selling root beer.

82 **THE GREEN DOOR TAVERN**
   678 N Orleans St
   River North ①
   +1 312 664 5496
   greendoorchicago.com

Though it wasn't officially opened as a bar until 1921, Green Door Tavern existed as a grocery store (and likely a speakeasy) since the building was erected just after the Chicago Fire: 1872. Either way, this is one of the city's oldest haunts, with *tchotchkes* and signage to show for it.

83 **SIMON'S TAVERN**
   5210 N Clark St
   Andersonville ⑥
   +1 773 878 0894

Simon's wasn't an official fixture of the Swedish-rooted Andersonville neighborhood until Prohibition ended in 1934, but it's likely that its namesake, Swedish immigrant Simon Lundberg, was running a speakeasy via his 'grocery store' in the decade-plus prior. In wintertime, the bar serves traditional hot Swedish *glögg*, and in summertime, there's a slushie version.

84 **GREEN MILL**
   4802 N Broadway
   Uptown ⑥
   +1 773 878 5552
   greenmilljazz.com

Since opening in 1910, the Green Mill has been in the business of live entertainment. But during Prohibition, when part ownership fell to Al Capone's gangster ring, moving booze became the main attraction. Tunnels were dug from behind the bar to an adjacent building, through which bottles – and Capone himself – could move in the shadows of the authorities.

85 **CHIPP INN**
   832 N Greenview
   Avenue
   Noble Square ④
   +1 312 421 9052

A solid spot tucked onto a quiet residential street in Noble Square. The space has operated as a bar since 1897 (likely doubling as a speakeasy during Prohibition), and its small footprint is conducive to a jovial crowd down to shoot pool, feed the jukebox and, given enough canned beers, dance with the coat rack.

5 must-visit
COCKTAIL BARS

---

86 **THE VIOLET HOUR**
1520 N Damen
Avenue
Wicker Park ④
+1 773 252 1500
theviolethour.com

The city's premiere craft cocktail bar, opened as a spinoff of New York's famed Milk & Honey (right down to the 'house rules'), is still one of its very best. Reservations are a must for sit-down service in oversized armchairs. To stretch your dollars, book during the 'Golden Hour' of 5 to 7 pm when classics are 13 dollars.

87 **WEEGEE'S LOUNGE**
3659 W Armitage
Avenue
Logan Square ⑤
+1 773 384 0707
weegeeslounge.com

Named for the 1930s crime scene photographer Arthur Fellig aka Weegee, this dark, vintage bar comes alive with era-appropriate tunes and cocktails every night. Try your hand at the shuffleboard table in the back, or step into the garden, lush with beer hops in the summertime.

88 **SPORTSMAN'S CLUB**
948 N Western
Avenue
Ukrainian Village ④
+1 872 206 8054
drinkingand
gathering.com

Pitch-perfect cocktails at agreeable prices. A lovingly restored art deco bar. Friendly service. Excellent DJs. Cozy booths. It's tough to name a better bar than this one. Sportsman's Club typically offers a handful of daily cocktails dreamed up by whoever's behind the stick that night.

89 BEST INTENTIONS

3281 W Armitage Avenue
Logan Square [5]
+1 312 818 1254
bestintentions chicago.com

A neighborhood bar of the very best design. This lovably low-key tavern happens to serve incredibly great cocktails along with friendly service and the atmosphere to match. Its comfortable, well-worn vibes, inviting patio, and solid food menu keep the tabs open round after round, offering inventive original cocktails as well as favorite and long-forgotten classics.

90 THE AVIARY

955 W Fulton Market
Fulton Market [4]
theaviary.com

What happens when a thrice Michelin-starred molecular gastronomy chef opens a cocktail bar? Though there's plenty of pretence, it's warranted: this uber-modern libations lounge continues to win accolades for its inventive and quixotic libations. Drinks can be ordered à la carte, but it's more fun to try a tasting menu or flight.

88 SPORTSMAN'S CLUB

5 BREWPUBS
and CIDERIES

---

91 ERIS BREWERY & CIDER HOUSE

4240 W Irving
Park Road
Irving Park ⑥
+1 773 943 6200
erischicago.com

According to the legend of the Greek goddess for which it's named, Eris aims to 'throw an apple into the party' of more than 100 local breweries in order to cause a stir. Eris is just as renowned for its ciders and beers as its location in a century-old masonic temple: the extensive renovation was recognized by the state's preservation society.

91 ERIS BREWERY & CIDER HOUSE

92 BUNGALOW BY MIDDLE BROW

2840 W Armitage Avenue
Logan Square ⑤
+1 773 687 9076
middlebrowbeer.com

Beer and bread are the calling cards at this airy space, where oven-fired pizzas dominate the menu. For a glimpse into the owner's charmingly idiosyncratic mind, order the Soppressata + Hot Honey (or, Sunday Afternoon on a Patio in Bushwick in 2008), which pairs nicely with the popular Yard Work Kölsch-style beer.

93 PIECE BREWERY AND PIZZERIA

1927 W North Avenue
Wicker Park ④
+1 773 772 4422
piecechicago.com

Piece is so well known for its New Haven-style pizza, one almost forgets that it's been brewing its own lagers and ales since 2001. Toppings on the oven-fired, loosely Neapolitan-style pizzas range eclectic and all of them are finished with Pecorino Romano cheese, oregano, and olive oil.

94 CRUZ BLANCA BREWERY

904 W Randolph St
Randolph Row ④
+1 312 733 1975
brewpub.
cruzblanca.com

When a brewery is owned by a star chef like Rick Bayless, the food had better be good. And it is. Casual street fare like tacos, tortas and burritos blend with lively crowds, casual conversations and free-flowing taps of Mexican lagers, IPAs and more.

95 MOODY TONGUE

2515 S Wabash Avenue
Near South Sid ③
+1 312 600 5111
moodytongue.com

The culinary antics inside this dark, anonymous building are proof that brewpubs can be sexy. Serving an unapologetically upscale menu of oysters, duck, market-fresh fish and layered chocolate cake, Moody Tongue pairs its vast menu of beers with high-end food for surprisingly delicious results.

5 cafes for
SITTING A SPELL

---

96 **PLEIN AIR CAFE**
**5751 S Woodlawn
Avenue
Hyde Park** ⑦
+1 773 966 7531
pleinaircafe.co

Located adjacent to Frank Lloyd Wright's famed Robie House, this charming French-inspired cafe knows its espresso drinks, but there's so much more. Stay for hearty sandwiches, yummy hand pies, perfectly flakey pastries, and a nicely curated list of wines. If it's nice out, find a spot outside at the lushly landscaped communal table to people watch.

97 **HEXE COFFEE CO.**
**2000 W Diversey
Avenue
Parkway** ⑤
+1 312 525 2099
hexecoffee.com

Though it opened with the intent of focusing on cold brew for afternoon pick-me-ups, this unique spot has been embraced for its all-day espresso (and coffee cocktails), down-to-earth service, and housemade pastries and sandwiches. The indoor cafe is cozy, and the vast patio space accented with native perennials buzzes with pollinators in the summer months.

96 PLEIN AIR CAFE

98 BREW BREW

3832 W Diversey Avenue
Avondale [5]
+1 773 687 9498
brewbrewcoffeeandtea.com

This modern Mexican cafe serves a variety of espresso drinks made with family-owned Factotum Coffee Roasters, including *mochas* made with Mexican chocolate and hot Oaxacan-style *horchata*. Quaint and quiet, it's worth getting comfortable and staying for lunch: the sauteed mushroom torta with creamy *poblano rajas* is a must-try.

99 BOURGEOIS PIG CAFÉ

738 W Fullerton Avenue
Lincoln Park [5]
+1 773 883 5282
bpigcafe.com

Celebrating its 30th anniversary, this European-inspired cafe hasn't changed much other than improving the quality of its food. The range of espresso drinks is expansive in part to serve the neighboring university crowd, and when paired with one of the Pig's ridiculously large brownies, it's worth settling into a velvet-clad armchair or settee to treat yourself.

100 SAWADA COFFEE

112 N Green St
West Loop [4]
+1 312 344 1750
sawadacoffee.com

It's easy to walk right past the graffitied door to this all-day coffee shop/eatery. Operating from the front of a large dining hall it shares with Green Street Smoked Meats, Sawada serves a neat selection of espresso drinks and heavenly doughnuts. Stadium and communal seating and a great soundtrack make good reasons to stick around.

5 exceptional
ESPRESSO BARS

101 **CAFFÈ STREETS**
1750 W Division St
Wicker Park ④
+1 773 278 2739

This wood-grained modern cafe stocks local micro-roasters to churn out expertly made espresso drinks. *Matcha* and *ube* are menu mainstays, seasonal flavors rotate throughout the year, and a selection of housemade vegan doughnuts and gluten-free sweets line the pastry case.

102 **INTELLIGENTSIA**
AT: MONADNOCK
COFFEEBAR
53 W Jackson
Boulevard
The Loop ②
+1 312 253 0594
intelligentsia.com

Though it's not as fabled as the growing chain's original location in Lakeview, this spot, in the lobby of the grand Monadnock building, is very special. Designed to complement the Victorian-era skyscraper, this outpost features classic white marble, walnut trim, bronze hardware, and bistro tables spread throughout the space. The coffee menu is decidedly modern.

103 **FOUR LETTER WORD**

103 FOUR LETTER WORD

3022 W Diversey Avenue
Avondale 5
+1 773 360 8932
4lwcoffee.com

Beyond its friendly staff and exquisite reading table, the draw of this sweet little cafe is its tidy menu of micro-roasts – espresso, drip, and a handful of teas – and a lovely rotation of local sweet treats by independent bakers. The signal-flag mobile outside pays homage to the cafe's sister location, on the tiny Turkish island of Burgazada. On weekends, the garage next door opens to reveal Four Letter Books.

104 DARK MATTER COFFEE STAR LOUNGE

2521 W Chicago Avenue
West Town 4
+1 773 697 8472
darkmattercoffee.com

Though notoriously hardcore roasters Dark Matter eventually opened its 'Mothership' HQ a few blocks east, this location was its very first, opened in 2007. Boasting a long wooden bar, loud decor and even louder music, Star Lounge is ground zero for serious caffeine heads.

105 PASSION HOUSE

2631 N Kedzie Avenue
Logan Square 5
+1 773 698 6649
passionhousecoffee.com

At first glance, this micro-chain of straightforward coffee bars is nothing special. There are no gimmicks, no highbrow decor, no bragging rights. What rises above are very good espresso drinks built from mostly single-origin roasts, friendly staff, and simple, tasteful spots to sit and sip.

5 bars
HIDDEN *in plain sight*

106 DORIAN'S THROUGH THE RECORD STORE

1939 W North Avenue
Wicker Park ④
+1 773 687 9824
throughtherecord shop.com

Pop into the fluorescent lit record shop on this busy strip of North Avenue, follow the door to the 'listening booth', and you're on your way to this drinks den where local jazz-fusion and funk-forward acts take the stage four nights a week. On off nights, DJs take over the decks offering refreshingly unique soundtracks.

107 THE DRIFTER

676-678 N Orleans St
River North ①
+1 312 631 3887
thedrifterchicago.com

You'll have to traipse down a sketchy looking stairwell to discover this genuine relic from Prohibition's golden age. Tongue-in-cheek custom tarot cards spell out the night's cocktail selections, and one of the city's premier burlesque artists curates the entertainment.

108 GOLDEN TEARDROPS BAR

2101 N California Avenue
Logan Square ⑤
+1 773 770 3414
lonesomerose.com

A basement service entrance reveals this pitch-black bar with an attractively moody vibe. A neon sign advertising 'Weddings & Funerals' sets the tone alongside eight spirit-forward cocktails and a solid trio of draft beers. Diverse rotating DJs and occasional karaoke or comedy nights keep things interesting.

109 NIGHTSHADE

4359 N Milwaukee Avenue
Portage Park (6)
+1 773 647 1942
moonflowerbar.com

Portage Park's Moonflower, kitted out with plants, *pinchos* and soul music, is lovely on its own. But its subterranean sister bar, Nightshade, transforms a trip to the basement into an entirely different night out. Minimal lighting and dark walls set the mood for a modest menu of classic and original cocktails.

110 CONSIGNMENT LOUNGE

3520 W Diversey Avenue
Avondale (5)
+1 773 384 6273
consignmentlounge.com

At first glance, this cozy storefront trimmed in Christmas lights appears to be a secondhand shop. And it is... sort of. Part antique shop, part cocktail bar, Consignment Lounge combines its owners' love for vintage *tchotchkes* and community gathering spaces. A handful of cocktails and beers are on menu, and everything on display is for sale.

110 CONSIGNMENT LOUNGE

5 *perfect* **PUBS**

111 **THE GREEN POST**

4749 N Rockwell St
Lincoln Square ⑥
+1 773 754 0632
greenpostpub.com

The epitome of a welcoming public house.
Nine choice beers on tap, a trio of rotating
ciders and a bespoke gin and tonic round
out the drinks, while the generous food
menu offers crave-worthy hand pies and
upscale takes on traditional pub fare. Cafe
service starts at 7 am for early birds and …
fans of live-streamed international sports.

111 THE GREEN POST ⑥

112 DUKE OF PERTH

2913 N Clark St
Lakeview 5
+1 773 477 1741
dukeofperth.com

One of the few Scottish spots in the city, Duke of Perth plays the part. Worn wood floors, amber lighting, and a wood-burning stove create a cozy atmosphere, and a large selection of single-malt whiskys seal the deal. Fish and chips are the thing to eat: on Wednesdays and Fridays, they're all-you-can-eat.

113 OWEN & ENGINE

2700 N Western Avenue
Bucktown 5
+1 773 235 2930
owenandengine.com

Step inside this handsome two-story tavern, and it's easy to imagine you're in the British Isles. Rich wallpaper, dark wood, leather, and a roaring fireplace set the mood for upscale interpretations of classics: a delectable Scotch egg, flaky Cornish pasty with chutney and greens, bangers & mash with onion gravy.

114 HOPLEAF BAR

5148 N Clark St
Andersonville 6
+1 773 334 9851
hopleafbar.com

Dozens of beers, cider and meads complement this spot's time-tested menu of nuanced pub fare. Order the mussels cooked Belgian-style in Unibroue's Blanche de Chambly served with fries and aioli, or the famous CB&J: cashew butter, yummy fig jam and gooey raclette cheese perfectly fried on chewy sourdough.

115 THE GLOBE PUB

1934 W Irving Park Road
North Center 5
+1 773 871 3757
theglobepub.com

A true sports pub, the Globe brings locals together for international soccer games at all hours of the day and night. The international selection of draft and canned beers and ciders keep the crowd rowdy, while a random assortment of pub fare aim to please the masses.

5 bars with free
LIVE MUSIC

---

116 CALIFORNIA CLIPPER

1002 N California Avenue
West Town ④
californiaclipper.com

Thoughtfully restored to its 1930s-era grandeur and bathed in alluring red light, the bar oozes laidback cool. A steady rotation of tasteful bands and DJs grace the corner stage, and typically there's no cover before 8 pm. To drink: bottles and cans, plenty of non-alcoholic options, and a handful of lesser-known classic cocktails as well as originals.

117 CAROL'S PUB

4659 N Clark St
Uptown ⑥
+1 773 754 8000
carolspub.com

As the city's oldest (and only) late-night honky-tonk bar, Carol's is a Chicago original. Featuring live music most nights of the week, the bar draws a nightly crowd of regulars that look to have been frequenting the place since 1972, and fresh-faced twenty-somethings learning how to two-step.

118 THE TACK ROOM

1807 S Allport St
Pilsen
+1 312 526 3851
tackroomchicago.com

Tucked into a corner of the beautifully restored Thalia Hall venue, this little saloon features a single piano and just enough room for jazz combos and trios to entertain a small crowd. Open only on the weekends, the bar typically books jazz and Latin artists, and serves a small menu of cocktails, wine and beer.

119 THE WHISTLER

2421 N Milwaukee Avenue
Logan Square [5]
+1 773 227 3530
whistlerchicago.com

Though it's widely heralded for its stylish cocktails and welcoming atmosphere, this hotspot is just as respected for its nearly nightly entertainment. On Wednesdays, the bar's Relax Attack Jazz Series hosts an impressive rotation of local new-wave jazz artists. Additional free live shows– – typically jazz – are sprinkled throughout the rest of the week.

120 LAZY BIRD

AT: THE HOXTON
200 N Green St
Fulton Market [4]
+1 312 761 1799
lazybirdchicago.com

Below the bustling Hoxton hotel lobby is this sweet drinking den serving fresh takes on lesser-known classic cocktails, and then some. (There are 52 cocktails in all.) From Thursday through Saturday, the bar hosts local R&B, funk and the like playing to laidback crowds trickling in before and after dinner in the neighborhood.

5 BEAUTIFUL

drinks destinations

---

121 QUEEN MARY

2125 W Division St
Ukrainian Village ④
+1 773 697 3522
queenmarytavern.com

Built in the late 1940s, this virtual time capsule was shuttered in 1975 after its owner was widowed. Forty years later, the bar was restored to its 1940s grandeur: original wood paneling, bronze gilded trim, and the most extraordinary wooden bar. Peninsula-style, it's adorned with tealights and hosts exquisitely made cocktails inspired by the British Royal Navy.

122 3 ARTS CLUB CAFÉ

AT: RH CHICAGO
1300 N Dearborn
Parkway
Gold Coast ①
+1 312 475 9116
rh.com/restaurants

The most beautiful place to sip a glass of champagne is in the center of a luxury furniture store. The airy atrium at the heart of RH Chicago's location is brimming with charm, from the gently trickling fountain at the center of the space to the tufted sofas daring you to get even more comfortable.

123 THE OFFICE

955 W Fulton Market
Fulton Market ④
theaviary.com

One of the most refined cocktail bars is decorated like a beautiful bunker. With just 16 seats, this dimly lit, leather-clad cellar lounge is home to some of the most unique bottles in the world…and a hot fudge sundae to die for. Service is impeccable, tabs are hand-tallied on parchment paper, and the drinks are epic.

124 KUMIKO

630 W Lake St
West Loop ④
+1 312 285 2912
barkumiko.com

Billed as a Japanese 'dining bar' that measures cocktails and decadent small plates in equal importance, this pretty, candlelit dining room exemplifies the art of quiet restraint. The namesake *kumiko* woodwork – pieces of wood layered into patterned panels – draw the eye to the bar at the back of the room, while subtle partitioning adds privacy.

125 BILLY SUNDAY

3143 W Logan
Boulevard
Logan Square ⑤
+1 773 661 2485
billy-sunday.com

Antique photographs, Depression-glass tealights, and a beautifully restored pressed-tin ceiling are a few of the aesthetic details that make drinking at this upscale cocktail bar a sepia-toned treat. Named for the local baseballer-turned-evangelist, the bar is known for its high-end ingredients and rare collection of amaros, and each drink is presented in pitch-perfect vintage glassware.

5 WINE *bars*

126 **OUTSIDE VOICES**

3204 W Armitage Avenue
Logan Square [5]
+1 773 360 8896
outsidevoiceswine.com

With an exposed-brick interior that's been nested in a curious grid of blonde wood, this playful wine shop takes a free-spirited approach to wines. No region is favored over another; instead, the common thread amongst the modest offering of red, white, orange, rosé and bubbles is that they are all natural, low-intervention bottles.

130 ALL TOGETHER NOW

127 POPS FOR CHAMPAGNE

601 N State St
River North [1]
+1 312 266 7677
popsforchampagne.com

Bubbles are the main event at this lively lounge that's been serving locals for an impressive 40 years. Beyond champagne, there are sparkling wines from California and other regions, and a handful each of reds, whites, and rosés. Cocktails and even non-alcoholic options round out the menu.

128 WEBSTER'S WINE BAR

2601 N Milwaukee Avenue
Logan Square [5]
+1 773 292 9463
websterwinebar.com

One of the city's very first wine bars, Webster's has been around long enough (30 years) that it's long since outgrown its namesake address on Webster Street. What's remained consistent is its dedication to primarily minimal intervention wines, knowledgeable yet personal staff, and a growing menu of bites.

129 ROOTSTOCK

954 N California Avenue
West Town [4]
+1 773 292 1616
rootstockbar.com

Half wine bar, half neighborhood restaurant, Rootstock is small, dark, and exceptionally laidback. It serves way more than wine – there are several dozen beers, ciders and special fortified wines here, as well as a range of spirits – but the spot's dedication to lesser-known vintners keep the corks popping.

130 ALL TOGETHER NOW

2119 W Chicago Avenue
Ukrainian Village [4]
+1 773 661 1599
alltogethernow.fun

This bar/shop hybrid hosts flirty date nights, friendly brunches, or grab-and-go picnic fare. A refreshing variety of worldly wines are the throughline: from Slovenia to Michigan, nothing is off the table. Regional partnerships with cheese and meat purveyors are reasons to stay and open anything in the store.

5 VERY SMALL *bars*

131 **THE VICTOR BAR**
4011 N Damen Avenue
North Center [5]
+1 773 360 7049
thevictorbarchicago.com

More intimate than tiny, The Victor Bar is as dark as its cocktails are strong. The simple menu is divided into Shaken and Stirred, with a nice mix of standards (old fashioned, sazerac) alongside originals (Scotty Doesn't Know: scotch, averna, lemon juice, maple syrup), and a handful of French wines.

132 **MATCHBOX**
770 N Milwaukee Avenue
River West [1]
+1 312 666 9292
matchboxbar.com

With barely enough room to squeeze into seats, this cocktail bar dates back to 1945 and was recently restored. Fortunately, its menu still reflects the classics, built in the classic style: with powdered sugar and fresh juice. Shimmy into a seat and taste the difference in the bar's gimlets, Tom Collinses, and famously strong margaritas.

133 **SMALLBAR**
2956 N Albany Avenue
Avondale [5]
+1 773 509 9888
theoriginalsmallbar.com

Cozy but not cramped. Boasting one of the city's most impressive beer menus, there are varieties and flavors to suit every taste. Check the specials board or ask any of the friendly bar staff to recommend a favorite. Order a side of fried cheese curds, root for whatever game's on the TV, and kick back.

134 MILK ROOM

12 S Michigan
Avenue
The Loop ②
+1 312 792 3536
*lsdatcaa.com/
milk-room*

If you've strolled through the Chicago
Athletic Association Hotel, you've
probably walked right past this itty-bitty
boîte whose vintage stained-glass doors
keep it successfully hidden. Behind them
are just eight seats, a single bartender,
and a collection of some of the oldest,
rarest spirits in the world – with the
prices to match.

135 THE ALDERMAN

1163 W 18th St
Pilsen
+1 312 243 2410
*thealderman
chicago.com*

Tucked behind a side door at an
enormous party bar, this 14-seat cocktail
den is as laidback as its mixologist-host,
Lance Bowman. After a complimentary
welcome drink, inventive interpretations
of classics are up for grabs alongside
originals incorporating everything from
toasted marshmallows to palo santo. The
hip-hop soundtrack keeps the drinks
from coming off too seriously.

131 THE VICTOR BAR

EXILE IN BOOKVILLE

55 PLACES TO SHOP

5 BOOKSHOPS
for browsing

136 MYOPIC BOOKS

1564 N Milwaukee
Avenue
Wicker Park ④
+1 773 862 4882
myopicbookstore.com

A Wicker Park mainstay for as long as the neighborhood has been hip, Myopic is a mecca of more than 75.000 mostly used (and some new) books crammed into three creaky floors of floor-to-ceiling shelving. Fiction rules, but there are also generous sections of nonfiction, biography, poetry, art and music titles, and more.

137 THE BOOK CELLAR

4736-38 N Lincoln
Avenue
Lincoln Square ⑥
+1 773 293 2665
bookcellarinc.com

As much a community hub as a bookstore, this Lincoln Square institution features frequent readings and events, and houses a small cafe selling soup, sandwiches, salads, and beer and wine by the glass. Several local book clubs use the shop for monthly meetings, which are listed in advance on the website.

138 57TH STREET BOOKS

1301 E 57th St
Hyde Park ⑦
+1 773 684 1300
57th.semcoop.com

Duck under the red-painted rain shelter and head down the steps to this cozy garden-level shop that serves the nearby University of Chicago. There are plenty of arts and humanities titles here as well as various degrees of special interest, and a great kids' section, too. Don't miss the excellently curated shelves dedicated to Chicago.

139 EXILE IN BOOKVILLE

401 S Michigan
Avenue, 2nd Fl.
The Loop ②
+1 312 753 3154
exileinbookville.com

This packed yet tidy bookshop is denser than it looks. Browse new releases front and center, or wander through the dual rooms of stacks, including a small used section in the rear. Named for Liz Phair's breakout album, the shop carries a small selection of vinyl for sale, and the owners' personal collections provide the soundtrack.

140 BOOKS4FREE

2931 N Milwaukee
Avenue
Avondale ⑤
+1 800 570 3698
books4cause.com

Stocked entirely by donations from the surrounding neighborhood and city, Books4Free is literally a free bookstore. As the first location of the locally based Books4Cause nonprofit, this simple storefront helps to promote an organic circulation of used books into the community that needs it.

5 VINYL RECORD
shops

---

141 DUSTY GROOVE

1120 N Ashland
Avenue
East Village ④
+1 773 342 5800
dustygroove.com

It's come a long way since its fledgling years as an early internet online trader. The brick-and-mortar shop keeps expanding to serve the growing demand for vinyl, and given how many records the online shop moves, the in-person crates are constantly refreshed. Check out the record 'take-out' window, which predates the pandemic by 20 years.

142 LAURIE'S PLANET OF SOUND

4639 N Lincoln
Avenue
Lincoln Square ⑥
+1 773 271 3569
lauriesplanet
ofsound.com

Though there's nothing particularly special about Laurie's, its friendly, pedestrian approach to popular music – particularly indie rock and alternative – has won over generations of locals and keeps them coming back for new releases and more. If you're selling, be sure to avoid titles on the shop's 'Do Not Never Ever Buy List'. (The Eagles are on it…twice.)

141 DUSTY GROOVE

143 TONE DEAF RECORDS

4356 N Milwaukee Avenue
Portage Park (6)
+1 773 372 6643
tonedeafrecs.com

Specializing in its owner's favorite genres – metal, indie rock, classic rock, and a modest amount of jazz and soul records – this Portage Park record shop is as friendly as they come. New and used vinyl (and CDs, and tapes) are stocked in the bins, and an impressive variety of local bands play live in the shop each month.

144 RECKLESS RECORDS

1379 N Milwaukee Avenue
Wicker Park (4)
+1 773 235 3727
reckless.com

This mini-chain is such a Chicago institution, it's easy to forget it opened as a satellite of London's Reckless Records back in 1989. Like the London shop, Chicago's stores prioritize a mix of new and used vinyl and CDs, and are famous for their staff-written album descriptions included on sleeves. Watch for occasional in-store performances and signings.

145 SIGNAL RECORDS

3156 W Diversey Avenue
Avondale (5)
+1 312 380 5158
signalrecords.com

Owing to its owner's experience running local post punk-electronic label Chicago Research, this pleasingly minimalist vinyl shop specializes in rare and hard-to-find releases of those genres as well as experimental and industrial music. A handful of popular classics are stocked in the bins, too, as well as an impressive array of underground dance music from afar.

5 unique
SECONDHAND *shops*

---

146 DOVETAIL

1452 W Chicago
Avenue
Noble Square ④
+1 312 508 3398
dovetailchicago.com

This keenly sourced collection of
covetable home and gift items draws fans
from across the city and beyond. Owner
Julie Ghatan carefully arranges the tiny,
tidy shop into complementary displays.
A handful of local designers find their
way onto the racks, though Dovetail's
true calling is 20th-century vintage.

147 ROCK N ROLL VINTAGE

4727 N Damen
Avenue
Ravenswood ⑥
+1 773 878 8616
rocknrollvintage.com

Local musicians frequent this expertly
stocked shop for gently used guitars,
amps, percussion, and tons and tons of
effects pedals that beg to be plugged in
and turned up. The shop stocks all the
major manufacturers from Martin Guitar
Co. to Moog, and naturally, anything and
everything can be tested out in store.

148 RICHARD'S FABULOUS FINDS

2545 W North
Avenue

West Town ④

+1 773 943 0710

*richardsfabulous
finds.com*

Richard Biasi has been in the menswear business since his days at high-street retailers like Ralph Lauren and Neiman Marcus. At his neatly organized secondhand shop, dove-grey walls and vintage mirrors lend the space the air of a gentleman's dressing room, with racks of ties, stacks of caps, and a collection of vintage barware.

149 DIAL M FOR MODERN

1818 W Grand
Avenue

West Town ④

+1 708 268 2069

dialmformodern.com

Even casual mid-century modern fans get sucked into this sexy shop with tastefully arranged furniture. Walnut, oak, and leather-based pieces are polished to showroom quality, then put on display alongside vintage accessories like cameras, one-of-a-kind artwork and eye-catching accent lighting. Nothing stays on the floor for long, inspiring frequent returns.

150 LOST GIRLS VINTAGE

1947 W Chicago
Avenue

West Town ④

lostgirlschicago.com

Launched from a trusty 1976 Winnebago gutted and kitted out as a pop-up vintage-mobile, Lost Girls does not take the traditional route to selling retro threads. The shop's two brick-and-mortar locations are each painted as colorful as the wares for sale, and the Logan Square location features a bonus store dedicated solely to housewares.

5 ICONIC
Chicago merchants

151 MERZ APOTHECARY

4716 N Lincoln
Avenue
Lincoln Square ⑥
+1 773 989 0900
merzapothecary.com

Established in 1875 as a small drugstore
in the Swiss apothecary tradition, Merz
remains the city's go-to spot for European-
inspired health and wellness. An array of
naturopathic brands cram the traditional
shop's tall cabinets, and knowledgeable
multilingual staff attend to customers.

152 ALCALA'S WESTERN WEAR

1739 W Chicago
Avenue
East Village ④
+1 312 226 0152
alcalas.com

Frequented by denim heads seeking out
the vast selection of Levi's and Wranglers,
Alcala's is first and foremost a mecca for
traditional western boots and cowboy-
style hats. The cramped shop famously
stocks thousands of each, worth window-
shopping alone.

153 MACY'S

111 N State St
The Loop ②
+1 312 781 1000
macys.com

When Macy's bought out Chicago-born
Marshall Field's, it took over the iconic
Marshall Field and Company Building
on State Street, much to the chagrin of
locals. Fortunately, it maintained Field's
beloved traditions: the 45-foot Christmas
tree displayed in the Walnut Room
restaurant, charming animated holiday
windows, and Frango chocolate mints.

154 YOU ARE BEAUTIFUL

3368 N Elston Avenue
Avondale [5]
+1 312 623 8249
you-are-beautiful.com

It began as a short-run of 100 stickers distributed amongst friends. Twenty years and millions and millions (and millions) of stickers, billboards, tattoos, and an Oprah special later, 'You Are Beautiful' is a universal mantra of kindness and compassion. This brick-and-mortar retail shop and studio offers a peek behind the curtain.

155 VOSGES HAUT-CHOCOLAT

2950 N Oakley Avenue
Bricktown [5]
+1 773 435 0094
vosgeschocolate.com

Vosges is to Chicago what Ghirardelli is to San Francisco. The luxury chocolate brand is famous for its offbeat flavor combinations and deep purple, Victorian-inspired packaging. Its 'Chocolate Temple' HQ is on a dead-end industrial strip marked by signature purple bricks and intricate ironwork, and it's open to the public.

151 MERZ APOTHECARY

5 *classic* WOMEN'S *boutiques*

156 ROBIN RICHMAN
2108 N Damen Avenue
Bucktown [5]
+1 773 278 6150
robinrichman.com

A pioneer of Damen Avenue's strip of unique boutiques, Robin Richman still stands out. Look for the bird's nest-like sconce and intricate window installations and step into a world where neo-Victorian frocks live alongside decidedly fashion-forward pieces. Shoes, accessories and artwork round out the offerings hand-selected from markets the world over.

156 ROBIN RICHMAN

157 IKRAM

15 E Huron St
River North ①
+1 312 587 1000
ikram.com

This blood-red boutique is the most prestigious in the city: owner Ikram Goldman was for a time the stylist to First Lady Michelle Obama. The international duds on display are often exclusive to the shop, and the clientele are of a certain caliber. For people watching, book a table at the cafe on the second floor.

158 P.45

1643 N Damen Avenue
Wicker Park ④
+1 773 862 4523
p45.com

For 25 years, this expertly edited collection of designers near and far has managed to honor both household names and up-and-coming designers without chasing trends. Most of the pieces here are designed for everyday wear, though little details and refinements help them stand out.

159 FELT

2317 N Milwaukee Avenue
Logan Square ⑤
+1 773 772 5000
feltchicago.com

Established in 2015 by two longtime friends, this simple shop has made a name for itself by supporting emerging designers alongside long-established labels. A relatively sparse layout – simple racks lining either wall, accessories table in the middle – allow for plenty of room to browse and take a glance in the oversized mirror.

160 KRISTA K.

3458 N Southport Avenue
Lakeview ⑤
+1 773 248 1967
kristak.com

For more than two decades, this ultra-feminine boutique has welcomed fashion-forward shoppers from the surrounding neighborhood and beyond. The airy two-story shop has plenty of room to stock popular clothing labels as well as a well-edited selection of jewelry, bags, intimates and more.

5 UNUSUAL RETAIL *destinations*

---

161 FINE ARTS BUILDING

410 S Michigan
Avenue
The Loop ②
+1 312 566 9800
fineartsbuilding.com

One of the city's first steel-frame sky-scrapers, the Fine Arts Building has *almost* always been a home for artists. (It spent its first decade as the Studebaker factory and showroom.) Today, makers and healers, puppeteers and authors, bookstores and music shops co-exist with opera singers and dancers, and they all open their doors on second Fridays each month.

162 BUDDY

AT: CHICAGO
CULTURAL CENTER
78 E Washington
Avenue
The Loop ②
hi-buddy.org

Even when the Cultural Center's vast exhibition spaces are dark, Buddy is an excuse to visit. Some 300 local artists and artisans crowd the shelves of this gift shop with everything from limited-edition zines to honey made on rooftop pollinator gardens. All proceeds directly support the makers.

163 AMERICAN SCIENCE & SURPLUS

27 N Northwest
Highway
Park Ridge ⑥
+1 773 763 0313
sciplus.com

Established in the late 1930s to offset excess wartime wares, AS&S scratches a certain itch for bargain hunters, thrifters and the insatiably curious looking for little gizmos and whatnots. Nowadays, it's squarely focused on educational and scientific cast-offs, which means you can score a telescope or rocks and minerals kit for a song.

164 ANDERSONVILLE GALLERIA

5247 N Clark St
Andersonville ⑥
+1 773 878 8570
andersonville
galleria.com

A cross between a fair-trade market and a shopping arcade, this eclectic collection of independent retailers ranges from jewelry and accessories makers to people peddling pet collars and potholders. There are more than 100 vendors in all, many of which don't sell their wares elsewhere. In other words, shopping here can yield one-of-a-kind treasures.

165 FASHION OUTLETS OF CHICAGO

5220 Fashion
Outlets Way
Rosemont ⑥
+1 847 928 7500
fashionoutlets
ofchicago.com

It may seem odd to spend time near O'Hare when not coming or going, but these stores regularly lure locals for a day of retail therapy. Luxe labels include Burberry, Gucci, Prada and Versace; American standards range from Levi's to Tory Burch. Don't miss the art installations: they're curated by Johalla Projects, known for courting up-and-comers.

5 great places for
HOUSEWARES

---

166 JAYSON HOME

1885 N Clybourn
Avenue
Ranch Triangle ⑤
+1 773 248 8180
jaysonhome.com

Richly layered with a mix of new and reupholstered vintage furniture, whimsical accessories, textiles and more from designers familiar and foreign, this local favorite is incredibly fun to browse. Its famous warehouse sale, held annually, is the ultimate in steals and deals.

167 ESKELL

2029 N Western
Avenue
Bucktown ⑤
+1 773 486 0830
eskell.com

Founded as a women's clothing line and boutique in Wicker Park, this eclectic and original home decor shop shed its skin a few times before finding a home on the edge of Bucktown. Amassing two stories packed with everything from votive holders to vintage couches, the space is inviting and the prices are competitive.

168 SALVAGE ONE

1840 W Hubbard St
West Town ④
+1 312 733 0098
salvageone.com

Salvage One is where old vintage pieces go to die...and become reborn again, for a price. Stroll around the 60.000-square-foot, multi-level warehouse and you might come across a pair of Victorian-era sconces from a long-shuttered hotel, or a modern, cast-off fountain from a failed (or famed) artist.

169 RH CHICAGO: THE GALLERY

AT: 3 ARTS CLUB AT
RH CHICAGO
1300 N Dearborn St
Gold Coast ①
+1 312 475 9116
rh.com

Even if you're not in the market for a new sofa, this massive 70.000-square-foot space is a must-visit due to its provenance: a former arts club and social house for women. Painting, music, and drama were the 'three arts' drawing together residents of this jaw-droppingly gorgeous 1914 institution.

170 ARCHITECTURAL ARTIFACTS

1065 N Orleans St
Cabrini-Green ①
+1 773 348 0622
architectural
artifacts.com

Opened by an archeologist in the mid-1980s, this shop amasses an eclectic collection of antiques, oddities, and true artefacts, all housed in a 37.000-square-foot midcentury grade school. Plan to spend a few hours weaving through the rooms crammed with unique treasures, collectible items and rare finds. There's a bar for pausing between wings.

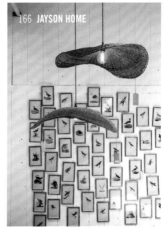

166 JAYSON HOME

5 WEIRD & WONDERFUL *boutiques*

171 BRIC-A-BRAC RECORDS & COLLECTIBLES

2845 N Milwaukee Avenue
Avondale [5]
+1 773 654 3915
bricabracrecords.com

This colorful and quixotic record and collectibles shop is totally 80s. VHS tapes, cassette tapes and vinyl are the media of choice here, largely dominated by campy classics that have aged pretty well. For a coffee break between browsing, check out The Brewed next door which oozes with horror-themed charm.

171 BRIC-A-BRAC RECORDS & COLLECTIBLES

172 WOOLLY MAMMOTH

1513 W Foster Avenue
Andersonville (6)
+1 773 989 3294
woollymammoth chicago.com

There isn't actually a woolly mammoth hiding in the corner of this playful shop of oddities, but there may as well be. Taxidermied animals, funerary masks, long-evaporated tinctures, handwritten postcards to long-dead relatives – there are layers upon layers to sift through.

173 SIDESHOW GALLERY

2219 N Western Avenue
Bucktown (5)
+1 773 276 1300
sideshowgallery chicago.com

Aptly named, this retailer stocks a lot of trinkets that don't quite belong anywhere else. Three-headed baby necklaces, tiny ouija board keychains, and artwork depicting the darkly occult are tastefully displayed. A curious rotation of events – tarot readings, broom making workshops, bone articulation – fill the calendar.

174 RR#1 CHICAGO

814 N Ashland Avenue
East Village (4)
+1 312 421 9079
rr1chicago.com

You could while away an afternoon just browsing, let alone choosing what to buy. The wares range from delicious imported soaps to light-up dinosaurs, authentic hand-stitched worry dolls to storybook-themed shelf puppets. All of it is fantastically layered and displayed.

175 JUDY MAXWELL HOME

1349 N Wells St
Old Town (1)
+1 312 787 9999
judymaxwellhome.com

This 'Genrl' store is located in a former porn theater on a charming strip of Old Town. Random personal items – fragrances, vintage lingerie – are mixed in with an even more random assortment of stuff: rubber baby hands, a Donald Trump countdown clock, drink coasters portraying celebrity mugshots. Its owner is actress Joan Cusack.

5 PLANT *and* FLOWER *shops*

176 **ASRAI GARDEN**
309 N Morgan St
Fulton Market [4]
+1 312 344 1467
asraigarden.com

Once upon a time, Asrai Garden was a little tiny cut-flowers shop on the fringe of Wicker Park. More than 20 years and a reality show appearance later, there are two locations blooming with gorgeous one-of-a-kind jewelry, timeless tooled-leather clutches, and so much more.

177 **SPROUT HOME**
745 N Damen Avenue
Ukrainian Village [4]
+1 312 226 5950
sprouthome.com

High ceilings and a thoughtful layout keep this well-stocked plant and housewares shop from feeling too crowded. Lesser-known houseplants and a handful of all-weather outdoor growers are beautifully displayed alongside an impressively designed 'dirt bar', a range of appealing terrariums, and an enviable collection of pottery.

178 **FLEUR**
2651 N Milwaukee Avenue
Logan Square [5]
+1 773 395 2770
fleurchicago.com

Plants in the front, housewares in the back, is how this neighborhood mainstay organizes its lovely array of offerings. A handful of offbeat cut flowers are on display for instant arrangements, while personal gifts and home decor lend a cozy vibe.

179 CORNELL FLORIST

1645 E 55th St
Hyde Park ⑦
+1 773 324 1651
cornellflorist.com

Voluminous, Victorian-inspired arrangements are the thing at this generations-old flower shop in a vintage storefront building in Hyde Park. Dating to 1939 with period architectural accents, the shop has an old soul but is decidedly modern. Beautiful ceramic ware, textiles and jewelry round out the gifts area.

180 PLANT SHOP CHICAGO

4601 N Elston
Avenue
Mayfair ⑥
+1 872 212 5827
plantshopchicago.com

There are no frivolous gift items in this sunny Mayfair spot: just tons and tons of plants. Friendly staff are on hand to point potential green thumbs in the right direction, and an emphasis on tough-to-kill varietals like succulents and tropicals make for lasting relationships for new plant parents.

179 CORNELL FLORIST

5 CARD and GIFT shops

181 **FESTIVE COLLECTIVE**

2643 N Milwaukee Avenue
Logan Square ⑤
festivecollective.com

Trips to this colorful boutique are sure to inspire your next party. The entire back room is dedicated to color-coordinated streamers, plates, napkins and more, while the lion's share of the shop stocks cheeky cards, adorable whatnots and local jewelry.

181 FESTIVE COLLECTIVE

182 PENELOPE'S

1913 W Division St
East Village ④
+1 773 395 2351
shoppenelopes.com

When its owners opened the decidedly clothing-centered shop, Gemini, next door, Penelope's shifted to serve other gaps in the neighborhood – stationery and paper goods, baby duds, and personal accessories, as well as a well-edited selection of clothing.

183 HAZEL

1835 W Montrose
Avenue
Ravenswood ⑥
+1 773 769 2227
hazelchicago.com

Founded in 2001 and expanded to a second storefront to carry men's and women's apparel, the original Hazel is still the neighborhood go-to for cards, gifts, and covetable personal accessories. Browse sweet baby gifts and cheery housewares, and check out the selection of Chicago-specific giftables.

184 KOMODA

2559 W Chicago
Avenue
West Town ④
+1 773 276 8229
shopkomoda.com

This cozy general store-like shop carries a number of hand-printed cards and stationery products, but it excels in personal accessories. Chunky ceramic necklaces, heavy brass rings and delicate bangle bracelets cover the display cases. There's a wide swath of personal care items, too, from international apothecary favorites to popular candle makers.

185 HUMBOLDT HOUSE

1045 N California
Avenue
West Town ④
+1 312 785 1442
humboldthouseco.com

This cheery, colorful shop oozes with good vibes. Cozy socks are neatly folded next to whimsical houseplant stakes; sweet earrings by popular local jewelry artists hang out next to indulgent chocolate bars. Don't miss the backroom with a great selection of home textiles.

5 great BOOZE shops

186 **HOUSE OF GLUNZ**
1206 N Wells St
Old Town (1)
+1 312 642 3000
thehouseofglunz.com

With its dark paneled wood, stained-glass windows, heavy draperies, gilded-framed portraits and candelabra sconces, the city's oldest liquor store resembles a Victorian-era library. Established in 1888, the shop stocks an incredible collection of rare wines and spirits as well as everyday bottles to pop for a casual picnic.

187 **MARIA'S PACKAGED GOODS AND COMMUNITY BAR**
960 W 31st St
Bridgeport (7)
+1 773 890 0588
community-bar.com

This former 'slashie' (half-liquor store, half-bar) was given a new life in 2010 when its second-generation owners built out a speakeasy-style bar behind the walk-in cooler. The liquor shop stays current with hyper-local spirits and beers, including in-house line Marz Community Brewing.

188 **VAS FOREMOST LIQUORS**
2300 N Milwaukee Avenue
Logan Square (5)
+1 773 278 9420
vasforemost.com

This no-frills liquor store rises above the rest for one reason: customer service. Established in 1957 as a corner tavern and packaged goods store, Vas Foremost offers a comprehensive catalogue of spirits, beer and wine. The tavern has long since closed, but the store has grown.

189 WEST LAKEVIEW LIQUORS

2156 W Addison St
North Center (5)
+1 773 525 1916
wlvliquors.com

Specializing in rare and hard-to-find beers, ciders, meads and perries. Domestic and imported bottles are neatly arranged in the cozy space, accented with a curated selection of books about imbibing. Another house specialty: single barrels of bourbon and rye from some of Kentucky's very best distilleries.

190 INDEPENDENT SPIRITS

5947 N Broadway
Edgewater (6)
+1 773 989 2115
shop.independent spiritsinc.com

Colorful regional maps and worn Persian rugs lend this modest shop an inviting feel. It's easy to linger when there's so much to read: most bottles are marked with neatly handwritten descriptions that are so eloquent, they've been analysed in creative writing workshops. Near the register, look for miniature chairs made from spent bottle cages.

186 HOUSE OF GLUNZ

FISHER STUDIO HOUSES

45 BUILDINGS
TO ADMIRE

5 historic
SKYSCRAPERS

---

191 THE ROOKERY BUILDING

209 S LaSalle St
The Loop ②
+1 312 553 6100
*therookery
building.com*

Completed in 1888 during the city's building boom following the Great Chicago Fire, this 11-story building was the world's first skyscraper. Renovated twice thereafter, The Rookery was touched by not one but four of the city's most storied architects: Daniel Burnham and John Wellborn Root, Frank Lloyd Wright, and William Drummond.

192 MONADNOCK BUILDING

53 W Jackson
Boulevard
The Loop ②
+1 312 922 1890
*monadnock
building.com*

Don't judge this historic skyscraper by its plain-jane exterior. Its solid, no-nonsense façade was a design choice when architects Daniel Burnham and John Wellborn Root were commissioned for the new commercial building in the late 1870s. Hiding inside are all the gilded flourishes common to the Victorian era – notably the decorative aluminium staircases that break up the long hallways.

193 RELIANCE BUILDING
1 W Washington St
The Loop ②

Designed and completed within the same timeframe as many other significant skyscrapers, this shiny corner building boasts one major difference: windows. The Reliance Building's repetitive ribbons of plate-glass windows lend it a lightness that wasn't evident in any buildings that came before it – but mark a distinct architectural feature in all of those that come after.

194 NEW YORK LIFE INSURANCE BUILDING
39 S LaSalle St
The Loop ②

Few buildings in the Loop epitomize Chicago's late-19th-century skyscraper like this one. Designed by William Le Baron Jenney as a 12-story structure, its classical combination of brick and terra cotta exterior is sturdy and reassuring. Inside, immaculately maintained Georgia grey marble lines the lobby and a beautiful grand staircase toward the west end of the building.

195 LUDINGTON BUILDING
1104 S Wabash Avenue
The Loop ②

As one of the earliest steel-framed skyscrapers in the city, architect William Le Baron Jenney's Ludington Building is a living pioneer. Two ornate Corinthian-inspired columns flank the entrance, and a series of equally ornate supporting stonework frame the oversized window panes.

5 ICONIC *buildings*

196 MARINA CITY

300 N State St
River North ①
+1 312 222 1111
marina-city.com

Nicknamed the 'corncob towers', architect Bertrand Goldberg's mixed-use development overlooking the Chicago River is home to nearly 900 unique condominiums with virtually no square corners. Upon completion in 1968, Marina City was the tallest residential structure in the world. Captured on the cover of local alt-rock band Wilco's 2002 album *Yankee Hotel Foxtrot*, it became famous anew.

197 CARBIDE & CARBON BUILDING

230 N Michigan Avenue
The Loop ②

Designed by the sons of seminal Chicago architect and planner Daniel Burnham, this is the city's most beautiful representation of art deco architecture. The 1929 building's decorative elements pay homage to its original tenants in the minerals industry: along the façade, dark green terra cotta with gold leaf referenced the ancient origins of carbon deposits in prehistoric plants.

198 TRIBUNE TOWER

435 N Michigan
Avenue
Magnificent Mile ①
+1 312 967 3700
tribunetower.com

Winner of a 1922 design competition to honor the Chicago Tribune's 75th anniversary, this neo-Gothic tower was until recently the headquarters of the city's premier daily newspaper. At ground level, look for 140 odd stones and rocks nicked from global landmarks – the Great Pyramid, the Alamo, the Great Wall of China – brought back from reporters' trips at the request of a former publisher.

199 THE MART

222 Merchandise
Plaza
Merchandise Mart ①
+1 800 677 6278
themart.com

When it opened in 1930 as a four-million-square-foot wholesale warehouse, the Merchandise Mart was the largest building in the world. In fact, it had its own zip code until 2008 when surrounding buildings began sharing it, too. Browse the showrooms for upscale furnishings trades, or stop into the food court for lunch.

200 S.R. CROWN HALL

3360 S State St
Bronzeville ⑦
+1 312 567 3230
miessociety.org

Modernist architect Ludwig Mies van der Rohe designed more buildings in Chicago than anywhere else in the world, most of which are on the Illinois Institute of Art campus, where he was the inaugural head of the architecture department. This self-described 'masterpiece' of steel and glass is one of the architect's best known structures. With no visible roof lines, it epitomizes his catchphrase: "Less is more".

5 examples of
21ST-CENTURY ARCHITECTURE

---

201 AQUA TOWER
BY STUDIO GANG
225 N Columbus
Drive
New East Side ②
+1 312 278 2782
studiogang.com

Completed in 2009 and standing
80 stories amidst the city's tallest
buildings, this tastefully modern
building is a refreshing break in
a skyline crowded with post-modern
skyscrapers. Designed by Jeanne Gang,
the wave-patterned building houses
the 18-story Radisson Blu and scores of
private residences that benefit from the
building's thoughtfully elongated terraces
with Lake Michigan views.

202 VISTA TOWER
BY STUDIO GANG
363 E Wacker Drive
New East Side ②
studiogang.com

Clad in beautiful glass plates that reflect
the passing weather, this is the tallest
structure in the world designed by
a woman. Similar to her Aqua Tower
a block west, architect Jeanne Gang's
Vista Tower evokes subtle curves that
bring a softness to the angular skyline.
There are three towers in all, gathered
like stems in a vase.

203 THE MODERN WING AT ART INSTITUTE OF CHICAGO

BY RENZO PIANO

159 E Monroe St
Millennium Park ②
+1 312 443 3600
artic.edu

When locals learned that modern architect Renzo Piano would be adding a wing to the century-old Art Institute, scepticism abounded. The result beautifully expanded the museum's area to one million square feet with an entrance (and, practically, a museum) all its own. To get a closer look, walk the bridgeway from Millennium Park to the museum's public terrace.

204 JAY PRITZKER PAVILION AND BP BRIDGE

BY FRANK GEHRY

201 E Randolph St
Millennium Park ②
+1 312 742 1168
jaypritzker
pavilion.com

One look at these shiny metal structures and it's easy to spot Frank Gehry's handiwork. Both opened in 2004 as part of Millennium Park, which reimagined a swath of rail yards and parking lots as a new 'front yard' to the city. In summer, the pavilion hosts live music while the bridge connects crowds to the sprawling Maggie Daley Park.

205 IIT MCCORMICK TRIBUNE CAMPUS CENTER

BY REM KOOLHAAS / OMA

3201 S State St
Bronzeville ⑦
+1 312 567 3075
iit.edu

Fans of Dutch architect Rem Koolhaas make pilgrimages to this Bronzeville campus to experience the futuristic, orange-accented cocoon-like structure. Encapsulating a small stretch of the Green Line El train to reduce noise pollution in the campus center, the building exterior mimics corrugated metal. Inside, everything from the grand stairway to the urinals are worth spying.

5 buildings
WORTH THE DETOUR

206 EDITH FARNSWORTH HOUSE

14520 River Road
Plano
+1 630 552 0052
edithfarnsworth house.org

Designed by Mies van der Rohe as a quiet country retreat, this glass-and-steel structure reflects the modern architect's signature style. It's situated on a sparse piece of acreage that yields all attention to the building itself, and the fully restored 1951 interior is open for tours five days a week.

207 BAHA'I HOUSE OF WORSHIP

100 Linden Avenue
Wilmette
+1 847 853 2300
bahai.us

One of just 14 Baha'i temples in the world (and the only one in the United States), this intricate, dome-roofed structure was designed by Louis Bourgeois and completed in 1951 after 30 years of construction. In accordance with the Baha'i style, the nine-sided temple is surrounded by a series of nine pathways, all of which are surrounded by nine gardens.

208 FRANK LLOYD WRIGHT HOME & STUDIO

951 Chicago Avenue
Oak Park
+1 312 994 4000
flwright.org

If you're even remotely interested in the work of prolific Chicago architect Frank Lloyd Wright, book an eye-opening tour of his home and studio. The exterior details of the adjoined buildings reflect the architect's fondness for prairie-inspired ornamentation, and the interiors have been completely restored to their 1909 state – the last year the Wrights were in residence.

209 HOLY TRINITY ORTHODOX CATHEDRAL

1121 N Leavitt St
Ukrainian Village ④
+1 773 486 6064
holytrinitycathedral.net

The famed architect and 'father of sky-scrapers' Louis Sullivan built only two churches in his 50-year career, and this is one of them. Tucked onto a quiet residential street in the charming Ukrainian Village, the quaint cathedral features an octagonal dome and storybook bell tower, among other Eastern European flourishes. Tours are held most Saturday afternoons.

210 ROBIE HOUSE

5757 S Woodlawn Avenue
Hyde Park ⑦
+1 312 994 4000
flwright.org

One of the best-preserved examples of Frank Lloyd Wright's prairie style of architecture, this is a rare opportunity to tour a nearly complete restoration. Narrowly saved from a bulldozer in the 1950s, the home was restored in the early aughts to its original style in 1910: the year the Robies moved in.

5 *buildings that* SURVIVED THE GREAT CHICAGO FIRE *of 1871*

211 **CHICAGO WATER TOWER AND PUMPING STATION**
806 N Michigan Avenue
Magnificent Mile [1]
architecture.org

When the city's premiere water tower was completed in 1869 to house boring old machinery, no one could have guessed how iconic it would become. After the fire ravished the entire downtown area, it remained intact. Ironically, the roof of the adjacent pumping station caught on fire, rendering it useless as a water source.

212 **BELLINGER'S COTTAGE**
2121 N Hudson Avenue
Lincoln Park [5]

According to legend, when he saw the fire drawing closer, Richard Bellinger cleared his property of dry leaves and tore up what he could of the wooden sidewalk, his picket fence and front stoop, then wet down his cottage with buckets of water. It worked.

213 **ST. JAMES CATHEDRAL**
65 E Huron St
River North [1]
+1 312 787 7360
saintjamescathedral.org

This grand cathedral has been through a few renovations over its nearly 200-year history, including one just before the fire. Built as a simple brick church in 1837, a grand redecoration was completed in the fall of 1871...and burnt to the ground save for the stone walls, a Civil War memorial, and an iconic bell tower.

214 ST. MICHAEL CHURCH

1633 N Cleveland Avenue
Old Town ①
+1 312 642 2498
st-mikes.org

To say this 1850s church 'survived' the fire is a bit generous. In reality, the building's wooden infrastructure burned to the ground, but its brick façade and stone walls stood against the heat. When the smoke cleared, they were the only structural elements that remained standing in this near north neighborhood. Rebuilding began just a week later.

215 OLD ST. PATRICK'S CHURCH

700 W Adams St
West Loop Gate ④
+1 312 648 1021
oldstpats.org

The city's oldest church – and oldest public building – was erected in 1856. Unlike other Midwestern churches of the era that utilized wood framing and brick exterior, St. Pat's was built with signature yellow Midwestern brick, which acted like a forcefield against the fire. Today, it's just as well known for its massive annual block party as its historic legacy.

214 ST. MICHAEL CHURCH

5 HAUNTED *places*

216 JANE ADDAMS HULL-HOUSE MUSEUM

800 S Halsted St
Near West Side ④
+1 312 413 5353
hullhousemuseum.org

There were no grisly murders or mysterious deaths in this well-known settlement house, but ghost tales persist – oh, and a side theory that the courtyard fountain is a portal to Hell. The most famous story dates to 1913, when Addams was confronted by neighbors demanding to see a 'devil baby' allegedly banished to the attic. Descriptive details included 'cloven hoofs, his pointed ears and diminutive tail'.

217 THE RED LION PUB

2446 N Lincoln Avenue
Lincoln Park ⑤
+1 773 883 2422
redlionchicago.com

Since it opened as an English pub in the 1980s (the building dates to the 1880s), some half-dozen ghosts have come in and out of its patrons' nights out. The most recognizable are a dishevelled looking cowboy and a 'lavender lady' whose scent occasionally permeates the upstairs area near the ladies' room.

218 ENGLEWOOD POST OFFICE

611 W 63rd St
Englewood ⑦
+1 800 275 8777

Credited as the country's first serial killer, H.H. Holmes operated a drugstore business out of a building of his own design that was rumored to have a crematorium in the basement. Nicknamed by tabloids as a 'Murder Castle', Holmes's building sat adjacent to this modern day post office, whose employees have mentioned feeling uneasy in the basement.

219 GLESSNER HOUSE

1800 S Prairie Avenue
Prairie District ③
+1 312 326 1480
glessnerhouse.org

Fortress-like and grand, the Glessner mansion was designed in 1885 by prominent Chicago architect Henry Hobson Richardson and construction was completed two years later – but he died before seeing the day. In tribute, the Glessners hung his portrait in the main foyer, and his ghost has been known to pass through to admire his work.

220 COUCH PLACE

24 W Randolph St, alley
The Loop ②

Known as 'Death Alley', this brick pedestrian way behind the Nederlander Theater was used as a make-shift morgue after the city's deadly Iroquois Theatre Fire of 1903. As firefighters searched rubble for survivors, they piled perished bodies in the alley. To this day, passers-by report feeling cold hands on their shoulders and hearing whispers.

5 **FAMOUS** *homes*

221 SAMUEL MAYO NICKERSON MANSION

737 N Michigan Avenue
Magnificent Mile ①
+1 312 641 5772
driehausfoundation.org

Better known as the Driehaus Museum in honor of the man that sponsored its 21st-century restoration, this 1883 landmark represents Chicago's gilded age in all its glory. Built as one of the city's premier 'fireproof residences' following the Great Chicago Fire, the mansion's write-ups in the papers of its time declared it 'The Marble Palace'.

222 ROGER BROWN HOME AND STUDIO

1926 N Halsted St
Ranch Triangle ⑤
+1 773 929 2452
saic.edu

As a prominent member of the famed Chicago Imagists, Roger Brown and his partner, George Veronda, were avid collectors of art and objects from a vast cross-section of cultures and nations. When Brown died, he donated his 1888 Lincoln Park building to the School of the Art Institute, which offers private tours.

223 GLASNER STUDIO

1366 N Sedgwick St
Old Town ①
+1 312 690 7359
edgarmiller.org

A craftsman through and through, Edgar Miller and his prolific legacy of woodwork, stained-glass work and sculptures are scattered across hundreds of buildings and homes throughout Chicago and beyond. The Glasner Studio, which Miller designed and crafted for R.W. Glasner in 1932, is considered his crowning achievement and known by Miller admirers as 'the handmade home'.

224 CHARNLEY-PERSKY HOUSE MUSEUM

1365 N Astor Place
Gold Coast ①
+1 312 573 1365
architecture.org

Designed by the ultimate Chicago power-couple – Louis Sullivan and Frank Lloyd Wright – this Gold Coast residence was completed in 1892 as a drastic departure from the Victorian designs of the day. Featuring a simple, unadorned façade, soothing symmetry within, and tastefully ornate details woven into the interior design, the Charnley-Persky House Museum is open for tours.

225 IDA B. WELLS-BARNETT HOUSE

3624 S Martin Luther
King Drive
Douglas ⑦

Home to the outspoken journalist and civil rights activist and her lawyer husband, this three-story Romanesque Revival structure was built in 1889 during the construction boom following the Great Chicago Fire. Wells lived here until 1929, after which it was divided into apartments, and later put on the register of historic places. Presently, the home is private.

5 *fabulous* FOYERS

226 TRIBUNE TOWER

435 N Michigan
Avenue
Magnificent Mile ①
+1 312 967 3700
tribunetower.com

Once home to the eponymous newspaper, this glorious neo-Gothic tower maintains the original lobby through which journalists passed for nearly 100 years. The centerpiece is a topographical map of the USA, and the walls are etched with quotes like this one from Abraham Lincoln: "Let the people know the facts and the country will be safe."

227 PENDRY

AT: CARBIDE &
CARBON BUILDING
230 N Michigan
Avenue
The Loop ②
+1 312 777 9000
pendrychicago.com

Opulence. Luxury. Success. These are the words that immediately come to mind after stepping into the lobby of this iconic art deco building. Though the lobby isn't finished in 24-karat gold (the building's tower is), its pricey Belgian marble, frosted-glass fixtures and gilded details are a feast for the eyes.

228 THE ROOKERY BUILDING

209 S LaSalle St
The Loop ②
+1 312 553 6100
therookerybuilding.com

It's all about that stairwell. Though the building was completed in 1888, its 1930s updates continue to lure visitors to the famous Light Court Lobby. Lofted into two stories, the space maintains its original, intricate ironwork, and features showy bronze elevators etched with beautiful birds of the art deco style.

229 LYRIC OPERA OF CHICAGO

20 N Wacker Drive
The Loop (2)
+1 312 827 5600
lyricopera.org

The epitome of gloriously gilded, over-the-top decor. During the building's extensive restoration of 1996, nearly 2000 gallons of gold paint were used. Follow the fluted, 40-foot-high Roman columns to the stenciled ceilings, then back down the Austrian crystal chandeliers illuminating the grand double-staircase, and the feminine pink-and-grey marble floor.

230 ELKS NATIONAL MEMORIAL AND HEADQUARTERS

2570 N Lakeview Avenue
Lincoln Park (5)
+1 773 755 4728
elks.org/memorial

This stately, domed beaux-arts building is recognized as one of the most grand memorials in the world. Cross the threshold of the 20-foot arched bronze doorway, and it's no wonder. There are 27 different types of marble sourced from around the world, all gleaming with natural light from the series of clerestory stained-glass windows.

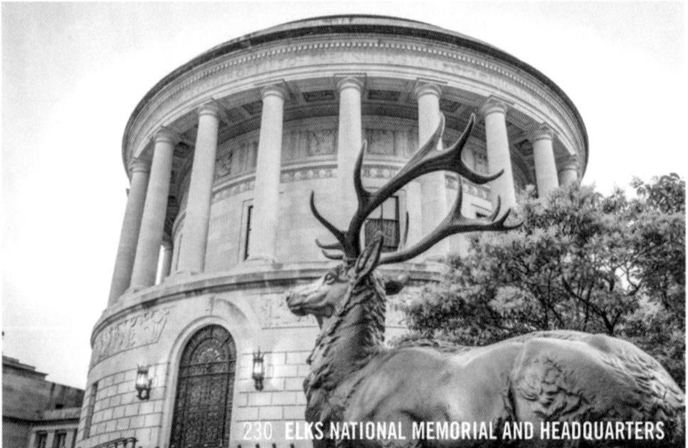
230 ELKS NATIONAL MEMORIAL AND HEADQUARTERS

5 EYE-CATCHING

structures

---

231 ALL SAINTS EPISCOPAL CHURCH AND RECTORY

4550 N Hermitage
Avenue
Ravenswood ⑥
+1 773 561 0111
allsaintschicago.org

Dating to 1883, this is one of the city's only authentic representations of the Stick style of architecture, featuring ornamental wood overlay mimicking exposed timber beams. Its use of wood is curious: post–Great Chicago Fire, new construction was required by law to be made from fireproof materials. Because this church fell just outside city limits, wood prevailed.

232 COMFORT STATION

2579 N Milwaukee
Avenue
Logan Square ⑤
*comfortstationlogan
square.org*

This quixotic little Tudor-style cottage is a vintage rest stop. In the early 1920s, a dozen or so 'comfort stations' were spread along the city's park boulevard system to serve passengers waiting at trolley stops. Fully restored in 2010, Logan Square's Comfort Station now operates as a nonprofit organization hosting art installations, performances and events.

233 CHICAGO VARNISH COMPANY BUILDING

55 W Kinzie St
River North ①

Situated on a busy corner in River North, this building often goes unnoticed even by locals – unless they happen to look up. Designed in a Dutch Renaissance Revival style and completed in 1895, this former varnish factory headquarters features an exaggeratedly pitched roof and a playful façade pattern of alternating red brick and light stone.

234 FISHER STUDIO HOUSES

1209 N State Parkway
Gold Coast ①

Commissioned in 1936 by Frank Fisher, a Marshall Fields executive, with a narrow strip of a lot and a wish for a dozen apartments fit for the upper-class. He hired local architect Andrew Rebori, who designed the apartment building in an elegant art moderne style; and craftsman Edgar Miller, who added unique design flourishes.

235 MYRON BACHMAN HOUSE

1244 W Carmen Avenue
Lakewood-Balmoral ⑥

This unique mid-century home sticks out like a sore thumb. In 1947, architect Bruce Goff remodeled the original late-1800s wood residence beyond recognition to suit the needs of its owner: recording engineer Myron Bachman. To convert the house into a home and studio, it's probable that soundproofing might have influenced the heavy exterior cladding.

234 FISHER STUDIO HOUSES

SKYLANDING BY YOKO ONO

65 PLACES TO DISCOVER CHICAGO

5 ways to ENJOY THE CHICAGO RIVER

236 CHICAGO ARCHITECTURE FOUNDATION CENTER RIVER CRUISE

MEET AT: 112 E WACKER DRIVE AT THE NE CORNER OF MICHIGAN AVENUE
Magnificent Mile ②
+1 312 922 8687
architecture.org/tours

One of the most popular tours with visitors is just as revered by locals, and for good reason. There's no better way to experience the Chicago River than afloat Chicago's First Lady, where personable docents from the Chicago Architecture Foundation point out the city's most notable buildings with spectacular detail while gently floating by.

237 CHICAGO WATER TAXI

6 stops along the Chicago River
Magnificent Mile ②
+1 312 337 1446
chicagowatertaxi.com

The most affordable way to experience the Chicago River from aboard a boat. Painted taxi-cab yellow and making six stops along the Chicago River from Michigan Avenue to Chinatown, the vessels range in size and can save time between destinations. Alternatively, bring a picnic and ride all the way to Chinatown's Ping Tom Memorial Park.

238 WATERIDERS KAYAKING

AT: EAST BANK CLUB
RIVERWALK

500 N Kingsbury St
River North ①
+1 312 953 9287
wateriders.com

A handful of kayak companies operate along the Chicago River, but Wateriders is the oldest and most reputable. Rent a one- or two-person kayak for a minimum of two hours – the perfect amount of time to go with the river's flow and check out the sites. Be mindful of boat traffic, which is busier on beautiful days.

239 TALL SHIP WINDY SAILS

600 E Grand Avenue
Navy Pier ①
+1 312 451 2700
tallshipwindy.com

The official flagship of the City of Chicago, *Tall Ship Windy* is a 148-foot four-masted schooner leading tours on the Chicago River and Lake Michigan. Unlike the city's handful of speedboat and tourboat offerings, this elegant sailboat is powered by the wind in the Windy City (though was built with a backup engine just in case).

240 KNOT MY BOAT CHARTERS

DOCKING AT:

3155 S Lake Shore Drive
Douglas ⑦
+1 312 971 0971
knotmyboatcharters.com

Grab a handful of friends and hire a captain. From May through October, it's fairly affordable to charter a yacht for the afternoon (or evening) with companies like Knot My Boat, SunSea Yacht Charters, Come Sailing, and more. Many companies offer a range of boat sizes to suit a dozen guests to 100, with drinks and catering services optional.

5 *beautiful* GARDENS

241 **ALFRED CALDWELL LILY POOL**

AT: LINCOLN PARK
125 W Fullerton Parkway
Lincoln Park [5]
+1 773 883 7275
lincolnparkconservancy.org

Tucked onto the east side of the park, hidden in plain sight between the Lincoln Park Zoo and its parking lot, this beautiful lily pool looks as if it was inspired by a fairy tale. Designed by Alfred Caldwell in a distinctively prairie style, the pool is open from spring through fall, with free docent tours on weekends.

242 **SHAKESPEARE GARDEN**

AT: NORTHWESTERN UNIVERSITY
East of Sheridan Road, South of Tech Drive
Evanston
+1 847 507 9416
maps.northwestern.edu

Though just outside the city limits, a trip to Evanston should always include a stroll through this beautiful Elizabethan-style garden founded in 1915 by the local garden club. Designed by Jens Jensen in a traditional English style with formal rows and straight paths, its features include a restored sundial, semi-circular permeter benches, and a stately memorial fountain.

243 LURIE GARDEN

AT: MILLENNIUM PARK

220 E Monroe St

Millennium Park ②

+1 312 228 1004

luriegarden.org

In peak summer, this vast modern garden is a sea of blue and purple thanks to its dense crops of sage, asters, blazing star, ironweed and more. Hidden from view by a dense 'shoulder' hedge – a nod to the 'City of Big Shoulders' nickname – it feels private and quiet despite its location between Pritzker Pavilion and the Modern Wing of the Art Institute.

244 CHICAGO WOMEN'S PARK AND GARDEN

1801 S Indiana Avenue

Prairie District ③

+1 312 328 0821

chicagoparkdistrict.com

This quaint park functions almost like a courtyard connecting a handful of historic homes in the city's Prairie District. The beautiful formal garden features tidy landscaping, neatly raked gravel paths, and a sculptural tribute to local activist Jane Addams. At the center is the Botanical Gardens Fountain, adding a tranquil soundtrack to the small space.

245 FORMAL GARDEN

AT: HUMBOLDT PARK

3019 W Division St

Humboldt Park ④

+1 312 742 7529

chicagoparkdistrict.com

When completed in 1908, this stately Formal Garden boasted year-round landscaping designed by seminal architect Jens Jensen. The garden features a semi-circular design and a central reflection pool – which has long been dry. A complete restoration project launched shortly before the pandemic, though is currently on hold. For now, just the garden's central flowers are maintained.

5 SCULPTURES
worth seeking out

246 ***THE WIZARD OF OZ STATUES***
AT: OZ PARK
2021 N Burling St
Lincoln Park [5]
+1 312 742 7898
chicagoparkdistrict.com

Author L. Frank Baum lived in Chicago while writing *The Wizard of Oz* series, and its famous characters – the Tin Man, the Cowardly Lion, the Scarecrow, and Dorothy and Toto – were sculpted by artist John Kearny from 1995 through 2007 and scattered around the park. Across town, Baum's home in Humboldt Park is commemorated with a mini-Yellow Brick Road.

247 **SHIT FOUNTAIN**
1001 N Wolcott Avenue
East Village [4]

There is no play on words here. *Shit Fountain* looks exactly like a perfect ribbon of poop, bronzed and placed on a pedestal in the form of a water fountain, bronze plaque and all. Created by local sculptor Jerzy S. Kenar in 2005 as a not-so-subtle reminder for neighbors to pick up after their dogs, it's quite a poopular – er, popular attraction.

248 *UNTITLED*
BY PABLO PICASSO
50 W Washington St
The Loop ②
chicago.gov

There are priceless Picassos hanging behind laser security systems in the Art Institute. And then there's this massive, 50-foot-tall sculpture sitting in a public plaza, where children happily slide down its steel wings with no consequence. Fondly nicknamed 'The Picasso', this sculpture broke tradition when it was unveiled in 1967 and has been winning fans ever since.

249 *SKYLANDING*
BY YOKO ONO
AT: JACKSON PARK
6033-6263 S Cornell Drive
Jackson Park ⑦
skylanding.com

Resembling a handful of silver lotus flower petals that happened to settle into the dirt, Yoko Ono's delicate *SKYLANDING* is the artist and activist's only permanent public artwork in the country. It's installed adjacent to the Japanese Garden in Jackson Park – the same site as the Japanese Pavilion from the Chicago World's Fair of 1893.

250 *FOUR SEASONS*
BY MARC CHAGALL
10 S Dearborn St
The Loop ②
chicago.gov

In the heart of the Loop, Chagall's intricate mosaic work captures the city in seasonal change marked by the human experience. Installed in 1974 and renovated and restored 20 years later to include a protective glass case, the mosaic reflects the artist's complex themes in even more detail than his famous *America Windows* at the Art Institute.

5 *pedestrian* **TRAILS FOR WALKING**

251 **BLOOMINGDALE TRAIL**

1805 N Ridgeway
Avenue
Humboldt Park ②
+1 312 742 4622
the606.org

Nicknamed 'The 606' after its throughline between the city's '606' zip codes, this ambitious rails-to-trails project is the longest of its kind in the country. Spanning 2,7 miles (4,4 kilometers) end-to-end, it's thoughtfully landscaped with native perennials and features a rubber jogging track as well as mile markers. It's wide enough to accommodate bikes, pram pushers, and runners.

251 BLOOMINGDALE TRAIL

252 LAKEFRONT TRAIL

Entrances along the
trail from Ardmore
Avenue to 71st St
Various ②
chicagoparkdistrict.com

Spanning an incredible 18,5 miles (30 kilometers) from Edgewater Beach all the way to the South Shore. The proximity to Lake Michigan is so close that in rough weather, parts of the trail are off limits. A recent expansion separated paved lanes for biking and pedestrian traffic, easing tension between the two.

253 312 RIVERRUN

Chicago River
between Belmont
and Montrose
Avenues
Irving Park ⑥

One of the city's newest pedestrian riverfront trails spans 1,5 miles (2,4 kilometers) along the North Branch of the Chicago River, offering car-free connections from Avondale up to Ravenswood. With fresh landscaping still in its early growth phase, over the course of a few seasons the paved trail should be blooming into a beautiful space.

254 CHICAGO RIVERWALK

11 W Riverwalk
Riverwalk ②
loopchicago.com

This 1,25-mile (2 kilometer)-long stretch of generous sidewalk along the Chicago River is populated with pockets of seating, quick bites, a handful of bars, and stops for the handy Water Taxi. In other words, it's not designed for workouts, but is very popular with the after-work crowd.

255 SAUGANASH TRAIL

4400 W Devon
Avenue
Sauganash ⑥
+1 312 742 7529
chicagoparkdistrict.com

Spanning an easy mile from Bryn Mawr to Devon Avenue through the lovely neighborhood of Sauganash, this wide, paved trail is ideal for quiet walks and bike rides. Sauganash Park, the halfway point, features a vintage fieldhouse and well-maintained tennis courts.

5 NATURE OUTINGS

256 LABAGH WOODS

West Foster Avenue
at N Cicero Avenue
North Park ⑥
+1 800 870 3666
fpdcc.com

Some 80 acres of dense canopy cover lend the combination of wetlands, savannas and meadows a genuinely rural feeling, and plenty of resident wildlife – from deer and mink to a range of birds and waterfowl – call it home. These woods mark the southern anchor of the North Branch Trail, a popular spot for biking.

257 SNORKELING NEAR THE SILVER SPRAY SHIPWRECK

E 49th St at
Lake Michigan
Kenwood ⑦

Chicago isn't exactly a diving mecca, but there are a handful of spots near the city to snorkel and scuba dive. The closest to shore is the shipwreck of the *Silver Spray*, which sank without fatalities in the summer of 1914 after hitting a shallow underwater rock terrain. Rusted in about 10-foot-deep water, it's easily accessible for exploration.

256 LABAGH WOODS

258 WEST RIDGE NATURE PARK

5801 N Western Avenue

West Ridge ⑥

+1 773 761 0582

chicagoparkdistrict.com

Fields of wildflowers, preserved prairie and a large fish pond make this North Side park a popular spot with locals of all ages. Its 21 acres are situated on the northwest side of massive Rosehill Cemetery – plenty of room for a web of paved walking paths, leafy trails, and even a little village of fairy houses.

259 NORTH PARK VILLAGE NATURE CENTER PARK

5801 N Pulaski Road

North Park Village ⑥

+1 312 744 5472

chicagoparkdistrict.com

Located within a uniquely protected woodland neighborhood called North Park Village, this roomy 46-acre area boasts miniature samples of Midwestern terrain: prairielands, an oak savannah, and wetlands. The coolest part is the park within a park called Walking Stick Woods: a 12-acre subdivision crossed with trails and natural play spaces set up for kids.

260 BURNHAM PARK

1200-5700 S Jean-Baptiste Pointe DuSable Lake Shore Drive

Oakland ⑦

+1 312 742 5369

chicagoparkdistrict.com

Often lost in the shadows of its more famous neighboring parks (Grant and Jackson), Burnham Park is a gloriously long stretch of green acreage with unparalleled views of Lake Michigan. Rolling green hills, modern bicycle bridges, a popular skate park and a massive bird and butterfly sanctuary are just a handful of the features that attract locals year-round.

5 delightful PARKS

---

261 PING TOM MEMORIAL PARK

1700 S Wentworth
Avenue
Chinatown ③
+1 312 255 3121
chicagoparkdistrict.com

Transformed from a former railroad yard, this serene greenspace hugs the South Branch of the Chicago River at the north end of Chinatown. Extensive paths and trails, a beautiful modern boat launch with kayak rentals, a peaceful pagoda, and three acres of native prairie habitat break up the space. It's the southernmost stop along the Chicago Water Taxi route.

262 ONE BENNETT PARK

456 E Illinois St
Streeterville ①
+1 312 662 1900
onebennettpark.com

This savvy two-acre park shares a design team with two other local favorites: Maggie Daley Park and the Bloomingdale Trail. Like those landscape gems, this mixed-use greenspace features a variety of materials to add aesthetic interest while defending itself against wear-and-tear. At its center is a lush lawn bowl.

263 WARD PARK

630 N Kingsbury St
River North ①
+1 312 742 7895
chicagoparkdistrict.com

A winding riverwalk, unique city views, and a larger-than-life engagement ring sculpture set this two-acre park apart. Named for mail-order tycoon Montgomery Ward, who fought to maintain public park space in the city amidst rapid development, it's tucked along a stretch of the North Branch of the Chicago River.

264 PALMISANO PARK

2700 S Halsted St
Bridgeport ⑦
+1 312 747 6497
chicagoparkdistrict.com

These sprawling 26 acres are a microcosm of the city itself. Risen from the ashes of a former rock quarry, the park features an active fishing pond fed by wildlife-rich wetlands, and paths of all shapes and sizes: recycled timber boardwalks, modern metal grating, traditional sidewalk, and even a crushed-stone running loop. Rolling hills give way to skyline vistas.

265 PARK NO. 474

3231 S Dearborn St
Douglas ⑦
+1 312 747 7107
chicagoparkdistrict.com

Though far too small to foster any recreation, this park has a famous inhabitant: a bronze cast figure sealed in white acrylic resin, forever seated on a wooden bench. *Man on a Bench*, sculpted by George Segal in 1986, was commissioned to celebrate what would have been local starchitect Mies van der Rohe's 100th birthday.

264 PALMISANO PARK

5 landmark
NEIGHBORHOODS

---

266 ALTA VISTA TERRACE DISTRICT

3822 N Alta Vista
Terrace
Lakeview ②
choosechicago.com

Inspired by the early-20th-century brick row houses of London, this quaint block features 20 different alternating exterior styles, repeating on diagonal corners so that the first house on one side is identical to the last house on the other side. There are 40 houses in all, lending the district its nickname: 'A Street of Forty Doors'.

267 PULLMAN HISTORIC DISTRICT

610 E 111th St
Pullman ⑧
+1 773 785 8901
pullmanil.org

When railroad engineer George Pullman sought to build a full-service plant for his burgeoning railroad sleeper-car factory, he purchased 4000 acres of land and built a company town. Established in 1880, it was the first planned industrial community in the country. It's since been swallowed by the city limits, and was declared a National Historical Park in 2022.

268 TERRA COTTA ROW

1014-1098 W Oakdale Avenue
Lakeview (5)

Embraced after the Great Chicago Fire to add embellishment to stone buildings, terra cotta was all the rage in the early 1900s. This tiny landmark district celebrating the golden age of earthenware comprises just four buildings along a single block, but the 'queen' of Terra Cotta Row, a Queen Anne-style residence at 1048 W Oakdale Avenue, is worth the trip alone.

269 BEER BARON ROW

Hoyne Avenue at Pierce St
Wicker Park (4)

Officially named the Wicker Park District, locals know this stretch of Hoyne Avenue for its massive Victorian mansions built by the city's wealthiest brewery owners of the late 1800s. Though the area was initially a cross-section of wealthy German and some Scandinavian immigrants, a later wave of Polish money earned it a nickname of the 'Polish Gold Coast'.

270 LOGAN SQUARE BOULEVARDS DISTRICT

W Logan Boulevard and N Kedzie Avenue
Logan Square (5)

Connected to a handful of other neighborhoods via famed landscape architect Frederick Law Olmstead's so-called 'emerald necklace' of green boulevards, this North Side district showcases mansion after mansion along grand, tree-lined boulevards and tidy central squares. At its heart is a roundabout with the Logan Square Centennial Monument, designed by Evelyn Beatrice Longman and topped by an eagle.

5 historic
MUSIC SPOTS

271 SUNSET CAFE

315 E 35th St
Bronzeville ⑦

This building was home to the Sunset Cafe, one of the most significant Chicago jazz clubs of the 1920s, welcoming cameos from Benny Goodman, Bix Beiderbecke, and Louis Armstrong. The building's interior walls feature a series of 1920s murals left from the club's heyday, which remained intact through its more recent years as a hardware store and beauty shop.

272 CHESS RECORDS OFFICE AND STUDIO

2120 S Michigan
Avenue
Near South Side ③
+1 312 808 1286
bluesheaven.com

Founded in 1950 by brothers Phil and Leonard Chess, the record label expanded into this building as its signature rhythm and blues sound launched the careers of numerous recording artists: Chuck Berry, Muddy Waters, Sonny Boy Williamson, Etta James, Willie Dixon, and many more. The building's address, '2120 South Michigan Avenue', was immortalized by the Rolling Stones.

273 RECORD ROW

S Michigan Avenue
between Roosevelt
and Cermak Roads
Near South Side (3)
bluesheaven.com

Beyond Chess Records, plenty of other midcentury nightclubs, recording studios, distributors and other businesses sprouted up as quickly as the hit records they promoted. The area's pioneering club, Macomba Lounge, was a launching pad for Chess Records; after Chess was established, many others – Vee-Jay Records, Brunswick Records, Constellation Records, One-derful Records – followed.

274 THE WAREHOUSE

206 S Jefferson St
West Loop Gate (4)

In the 1970s, a warehouse building at this spot was converted to a nightclub aptly named The Warehouse, and a DJ named Frankie Knuckles was invited to be its resident selector. Within a few years' time, Knuckles had landed on a unique style of disco and electronic music that his regulars began referring to as 'house music', named for the club.

275 ELECTRICAL AUDIO

2621 W Belmont
Avenue
Avondale (5)
+1 773 539 2555
electricalaudio.com

Chances are you own at least one record made in this modest two-room recording studio. Founded and managed by renowned local engineer and musician Steve Albini, Electrical Audio is the place where some of the most iconic musical artists in the world – from the Foo Fighters to the Stooges – laid down tracks that would eventually define their careers.

5 MAGICAL
experiences

276 CHICAGO MAGIC LOUNGE

5050 N Clark St
Uptown ⑥
+1 312 366 4500
*chicagomagic
lounge.com*

Find your way through the faux laundromat that serves as the foyer, and you'll wind up in the Performance Bar: the art deco-styled holding pen for performances at this intriguing nightlife destination. Purchase a pair of advance tickets to the Signature Show, which features nightly headlining magicians as well as openers.

276 CHICAGO MAGIC LOUNGE

277 THE MAGIC PARLOUR

AT: PALMER HOUSE
HILTON HOTEL
17 E Monroe St
The Loop ②
+1 312 300 6803
*themagicparlour
chicago.com*

As the long-standing house show at the historical Palmer House Hilton Hotel, this 75-minute live performance is both classic and classy. The resident entertainer is Dennis Watkins, a third-generation magician and mentalist with an impressive resume of award-winning theater performances.

278 MAGIC INC.

1838 W Lawrence
Avenue
Ravenswood ⑥
+1 773 334 2855
magicinc.net

Established in the roaring twenties as the Ireland Magic Company, this brick-and-mortar store is the longest continuously family-run magic shop in the country. Though it looks a bit dated inside, that's part of the allure. Memorabilia is mixed in with the magic, and signed playing cards adorn the ceiling.

279 MALLIWAY BROS

1407 W Morse
Avenue
Rogers Park ⑥
+1 773 754 7546
malliwaybros.com

As one of the city's newer shops peddling magic and the occult, Malliway Bros fosters a decidedly modern approach to the obscure. Stocking more witchcraft than magic, the space has an antique parlor vibe but is popular with the next generation of spellbound patrons.

280 THE OCCULT BOOKSTORE

3031 N Milwaukee
Avenue
Avondale ⑤
+1 773 292 0995
occultbookstore.com

One could spend hours browsing the collection of uniquely spiritual books at this newly relocated shop where magic (and Magick) is in the air. First established in 1918 on State Street serving as a resource for mysticism and mysteries, the aptly named Occult Bookstore is the oldest spirit shop in the country.

5 relics of
HISTORY

---

281 PICKWICK PLACE

22 E Jackson
Boulevard
The Loop ②

Other than a small plaque, there's scant evidence of all of the history packed into this tiny alley – from a two-story horse barn in the 1850s to a post–Great Chicago Fire brick building housing a string of restaurants. Today, the tiny ground floor hosts a coffee take-out window.

282 ROSEHILL CEMETERY ENTRANCE

5800 N Ravenswood
Avenue
Andersonville ⑥
+1 773 561 5940
dignitymemorial.com

If the entrance to the city's largest cemetery is reminiscent of the famous Water Tower downtown, that's because they share the same architect. Designed in the fantastic castellated Gothic style by William W. Boyington in 1864, the castle-like entrance welcomes visitors to its sprawling 350 acres of graves for Chicagoans of note.

283 CITY HALL FINIAL

2045 N Lincoln
Park West
Lincoln Park ⑤
chicagoparkdistrict.com

Sitting in a patch of grass as if it simply fell off of a truck, this ornament was salvaged from City Hall after the Great Chicago Fire. One of two dozen identical 1860s finials that lined the roof of the original Court House Building, it's sat here for more than a century.

284 CHICAGO FIRE RELIC

AT: CHICAGO HISTORY MUSEUM
Near 1601 N Clark St
Lincoln Park [5]
+1 312 642 4600
chicagohistory.org/history-trail

There's no way to describe this object other than as a giant chunk of molten metal. Discovered by a construction crew nearly 20 years after the Great Chicago Fire, this seven-ton mass of melted iron, brick and stone – the remnants of an iron warehouse – was so firmly lodged into the earth, the 1890s crew simply had to build around it.

285 CHICAGO MOTOR CLUB MAP

68 E Wacker Place
The Loop [2]
chicagology.com

Before Google Maps, there was the Automobile Association of America, or Triple A: a club to help drivers safely find their way across the country while sightseeing. Built in 1929, the former Chicago headquarters maintains a 30-foot map of the country pinpointing major highways and cities of the era. Today, the beautifully preserved building is a posh Hampton Inn.

285 CHICAGO MOTOR CLUB MAP

5 incredible **VIEWS**

286 CINDY'S ROOFTOP

12 S Michigan
Avenue
The Loop ②
+1 312 792 3502
cindysrooftop.com

With a delicious menu and views like
these, it's easy to see why Cindy's is one
of the toughest brunch reservations
in the city. Perched atop the historic
Chicago Athletic Association building
directly across from Millennium Park,
this greenhouse-like restaurant has a rare
vantage of the entire park, from 'The
Bean' to the Art Institute, and beyond.

286 CINDY'S ROOFTOP

287 THE UP ROOM AT THE ROBEY

2018 W North
Avenue
Wicker Park ④
+1 872 315 3060
therobey.com

A round of drinks at this dark and cozy cocktail bar comes with panoramic easterly views of the skyline, and the patchwork of neighborhoods in between. Perched atop the 13th floor of an art deco-era flatiron building, the outdoor patio leads to a secret stone nook built for two.

288 THE SIGNATURE ROOM AT THE 95TH

875 N Michigan
Avenue
Magnificent Mile ①
+1 312 787 9596
signatureroom.com/
lounge

This classy bar atop the former Hancock Center is famous for its miles-long views of the city looking west. Unlike many of the city's top observation decks, there's no cover other than the price of your drinks. Be sure to stop into the bathrooms: there you'll find an entirely different angle of the 95-story vistas.

289 THE ADLER PLANETARIUM

1300 S DuSable Lake
Shore Drive
Museum Campus ③
+1 312 922 7827
adlerplanetarium.org

Whether or not you have time to spend at the city's wonderful planetarium, making the trek to the eastern edge of Museum Campus on a clear day is rewarding. If you can, wait to take in the view until you've walked all the way to the end of the turnaround. Then, treat yourself to a stunning skyline vista.

290 CALUMET PARK

9801 S Avenue G
East Side ⑧
+1 312 747 6039
chicagoparkdistrict.com

One of the very best views of the city is on the Indiana state line. Due to the gentle curve of the southern shoreline from the Loop onward, Calumet Park is the furthest southeastern most point of the shoreline, which means that magnificent views looking back up at the skyline are clear as day.

5 LOCAL MARKETS

291 **TOTTO'S MARKET**
751 S Dearborn St
Printers Row (2)
+1 312 888 3600
tottosmarket.com

Everything in this cheery, sunlit corner market looks like something you'll want to take home. From the imported chocolate bars to fresh deli sandwiches, Totto's aims to feed the local neighborhood by any means, thanks to its friendly motto: 'You're a stranger here but once'.

292 **GENE'S SAUSAGE SHOP & DELICATESSEN**
4750 N Lincoln Avenue
Lincoln Square (6)
+1 773 728 7243
genessausage.com

There's so much more than sausage at this European-style gourmet market, a neighborhood staple for a half-century. The two-story shop boasts a traditional deli with meats cut to order and a variety of imported and locally sourced provisions. On summer weekends, the glorious rooftop beer garden opens for pilsners and brats with a view.

293 **JOONG BOO MARKET**
3333 N Kimball Avenue
Avondale (5)
+1 773 478 5566
joongboomarket.com

Locals flock to this jam-packed Asian market. There's an incredible selection of fresh fish cut and packaged by request, and the produce department stocks specialty greens that simply aren't found elsewhere in town. Wander down the aisles to shop a hefty selection of rice and seaweed products.

294 **OLIVIA'S MARKET**

2014 W Wabansia Avenue
Wicker Park [5]
+1 773 227 4220
oliviasmarket.com

This petite garden-level grocer offers such a thoughtful selection of fruits and veg, produce basics, and pantry staples, it's hard to justify making a trip to a big-box store for anything else. From nicely priced bottles of wine to a cheery selection of fresh-cut flowers, Olivia's makes the shopping experience charming.

295 **THE GODDESS AND GROCER**

1649 N Damen Avenue
Wicker Park [4]
+1 773 342 3200
goddessandgrocer.com

A local mini empire, The Goddess and Grocer got its start as a little sandwich and deli shop with delicious freshly made salads. Given the owner's background in cooking for and catering to rock stars, it's no wonder the shop stocks such a flavorful array of foods fit for discerning taste buds.

291 TOTTO'S MARKET

5 *Midwestern* **SPORTS** *to wait out the winter*

296 **DUCKPIN BOWLING**
AT: PINK SQUIRREL
2414 N Milwaukee Avenue
Logan Square [5]
+1 773 904 8185
pinksquirrelbar.com

Duckpin bowling is a mini version of bowling that happens to transfer beautifully to cozy Midwestern bars. Inspired by a legendary 'mini bowl' in Milwaukee, the Pink Squirrel's owner installed two tiny lanes in his throwback cocktail bar. The bowling – which utilizes squat, lightweight pins and small, heavy bowling balls – gets increasingly difficult with each delicious cocktail.

296 DUCKPIN BOWLING AT PINK SQUIRREL

297 CLASSIC BOWLING

AT: AVONDALE BOWL

3118 N Milwaukee
Avenue

Avondale ⑤

+1 708 816 1993

avondalebowl.com

This lovingly restored 1920s bowling alley features retro flair, including hand-scoring and the original wooden lanes. With extensive rehab work, literally everything was revived to beautiful working order, right down to the vintage Brunswick pin-setters. The only thing that's missing is the classic bowling alley smell.

298 ARCADE GAMES

AT: LOGAN ARCADE

2410 W Fullerton
Avenue

Logan Square ⑤

+1 872 206 2859

loganarcade.com

In a former hardware store building with a chequered past (for decades, the Chicago location of Southern Records was here; later it was a record store), this vast arcade bar houses one of the city's largest collections of classic pinball machines. An impressive drink list and lack of natural light make it easy to stay for hours.

299 SLOT CAR RACING

AT: RUN RABBIT RUN

3255 W Bryn Mawr
Avenue

North Park ⑥

+1 773 372 4309

The 1960s rec room pastime is back on track. Sparked by its owner's nostalgia, Run Rabbit Run invites patrons to pick their favorite tabletop racetrack, start their electrically controlled engines, and let 'er rip. A handful of vintage toy cars for sale liven up the space.

300 TABLE SHUFFLEBOARD

AT: THE GAME ROOM

12 S Michigan
Avenue

The Loop ②

+1 312 792 3535

lsdatcaa.com/game-room

At this lively and handsome rec room, table shuffleboard is just one of a half-dozen ways to pass the time. Just like the fair-weather leisure sport (but downsized to fit on a table slick with a special wax or sand), table shuffleboard is all about knocking your puck as close to the end of the board without overshooting.

50 WAYS TO ENJOY CULTURE

5 **S M A L L** *museums and institutions*

---

301 **SMART MUSEUM OF ART**
5550 S Greenwood Avenue
Hyde Park ⑦
+1 773 702 0200
smartmuseum. uchicago.edu

The University of Chicago's museum of art has grown in its 50 years to collect more than 16.000 objects. Recent exhibitions are decidedly modern, but the collection includes European works leading up to the 19th century as well as ancient Asian art. The building is centered around a quaint courtyard: the heart of the school's art history department.

302 **THE RENAISSANCE SOCIETY**
5811 S Ellis Avenue
Hyde Park ⑦
+1 773 702 8670
renaissancesociety.org

Established in 1915 as a forward thinking exhibitor of modern artists, this modest single-gallery museum lives in a beautifully annexed space on the University of Chicago's campus. From its start, The Ren, as it's known, has existed as a *kunsthalle*-style space, exhibiting seasonal shows and the occasional performance, but with no permanent collection to speak of.

303 UKRAINIAN INSTITUTE OF MODERN ART

2320 W Chicago Avenue
Ukrainian Village ④
+1 773 227 5522
uima-chicago.org

Considering the city's deep ties to Ukraine (Chicago hosts one of the largest populations in the country), it's fitting that there's a dedicated modern art museum in the heart of the Ukrainian Village. Established in 1971, this simple yet modern space hosts rotating exhibitions from the permanent collection and beyond, as well as film screenings, concerts, readings, and more.

304 STONY ISLAND ARTS BANK

6760 S Stony Island Avenue
Jackson Park ⑦
+1 312 857 5561
rebuild-foundation.org

A cross between a library, a community center, a gallery space, and an arts foundation, the Stony Island Arts Bank is truly one of a kind. Housed in a 1920s bank building purchased by local cultural icon Theaster Gates for a rumored one dollar, the building was thoughtfully restored to showcase wow-worthy archives of local Black artists.

305 MUSEUM OF CONTEMPORARY PHOTOGRAPHY

600 S Michigan Avenue
South Loop ②
+1 312 663 5554
mocp.org

There's always an engaging exhibit on display at this airy museum at Columbia College Chicago, which has accommodated increasingly more technologically minded works alongside the changing face of photography. In the main exhibition space, a rotating series of international visual artists are given real estate to showcase new work, often with built-in lectures and programming.

5 GALLERIES
and ART CLUBS

306 **WESTERN EXHIBITIONS**
1709 W Chicago Avenue, #5009
West Town ④
+1 312 480 8390
westernexhibitions.com

A longtime exhibitor of weird and wonderful, unique and thought-provoking works. Among the standouts are Deb Sokolow's tongue-in-cheek conspiracy plans, Paul Nudd's vaguely biological bursts of color, and partners Dutes Miller and Stan Shellabarger's beautiful collaborations.

307 **KAVI GUPTA GALLERY**
835 W Washington Boulevard
West Loop ④
+1 312 432 0708
kavigupta.com

Kavi Gupta represents a roster of artists on the brink of breakout, and maintains them through their success. Layer-rich painter Angel Otero, multidisciplinary sculptor Allana Clarke, and culture vulture Tony Tasset are among Gupta's diverse roster.

308 **THE ARTS CLUB OF CHICAGO**
201 E Ontario St
Streeterville ①
+1 312 787 3997
artsclubchicago.org

Set in a Mies van der Rohe-inspired building, this private arts club maintains a street-level gallery open to the public. International stars and local up-and-comers alike have staged traditional framed wall hangings, site-specific installations in the garden, and jaw-dropping takeovers of the gallery space.

309 CARRIE SECRIST GALLERY

1732 W Hubbard St, #1A
West Town ④
+1 312 610 3821
secristgallery.com

Though Secrist's roster of artists doesn't stray too far from painting, drawing, sculpture and collage, the exhibitions are anything but traditional. The gallery is known to paint gallery walls a stark aqua to help works pop, or install a yellow stripe on its floor to create space for abstract sculpture installations.

310 VERTICAL GALLERY

2006 W Chicago Avenue, #1R
Ukrainian Village ④
+1 773 697 3846
verticalgallery.com

On a busy stretch of this hip hood, Vertical Gallery packs in the crowds for dense exhibitions inspired by street art, pop culture, and highly graphic illustrations. Many works are grouped directly next to each other to maximize wall space, and the range of art – from graffiti writers to hyper-realistic painters – is a treat.

308 THE ARTS CLUB OF CHICAGO

5 ART INSTITUTE
hidden highlights

———

111 S Michigan Avenue
The Loop ②
+1 312 443 3600
artic.edu

311 PAPERWEIGHTS COLLECTION

How exciting can paperweights really be? Very, when they're museum quality. Most of the museum's collection dates to the Victorian era: the apex of flowery correspondence with an art object to match. Thanks to a paperweight renaissance in the 1970s, there are a handful of modern weights among the 1400 total.

312 THORNE MINIATURE ROOMS

There are doll houses, and then there are Narcissa Niblack Thorne's miniature rooms: precise 1:12 scale reproductions as specific as the 'English Bedchamber of the Jacobean or Stuart Period, 1603–88', complete with faux leaded-glass and wood-paneled ceilings. No larger than a shoebox, each room was designed by Thorne in the 1930s and painstakingly crafted by nimble-fingered artisans.

313 SOUTH GARDEN

Few spots in the Loop are as serene as the lush courtyard garden directly south of the museum's historic wing. During warm months, 9-to-5-ers stretch their legs and take in al fresco lunches while the garden's water feature, sculptor Loredo Taft's *Fountain of the Great Lakes*, bubbles for an audience of locust and hawthorn trees.

314 STOCK EXCHANGE TRADING ROOM

Dating to 1894 and salvaged from demolition in the 1970s, this stunning room is a must-see for fans of seminal architect Louis Sullivan. Everything is intact, from the plaster moulding to the art glass and those impossibly intricate stencils lining the walls. It's technically not open to the public, but museum guards are known to oblige.

315 ARMS AND ARMOR COLLECTION

On a dead-end of the second floor, shrouded in a dark-lit gallery is a window into the warfare of the past. It's fascinating to see not only the craftsmanship of full body armor made some 600 years ago, but also the approximate stature of the people that would have worn it. One primitive sword dates to 1200.

5 UNIQUE
museums and institutions

316 **BUSY BEAVER BUTTON MUSEUM**
3407 W Armitage Avenue
Logan Square [5]
+1 773 645 3359
buttonmuseum.org

Have you ever considered the pinback button? Local button aficionados and siblings Christen and Joel Carter are the curators behind this humble museum, located inside the Busy Beaver Button Company. The collection has grown to an incredible 55.000 buttons, the oldest of which dates back to a stamped-metal button from George Washington's inauguration in 1789.

317 INTUIT: THE CENTER FOR INTUITIVE AND OUTSIDER ART

317 INTUIT: THE CENTER FOR INTUITIVE AND OUTSIDER ART

756 N Milwaukee Avenue
River West ①
+1 312 624 9487
art.org

By far one of the most fascinating art museums in the city. Intuit spotlights self-taught artists whose talent, for whatever reason, wasn't recognized while they were alive. The result is an incredibly eclectic collection of art pieces and styles with a refreshingly unique perspective.

318 INTERNATIONAL MUSEUM OF SURGICAL SCIENCE

1524 N Lake Shore Drive
Gold Coast ①
+1 312 642 6502
imss.org

Housed in the Countiss Mansion – a 1917 building modeled after Marie Antoinette's private chateau – this is the most architecturally beautiful and artifactually bizarre museum in the city. Showcasing a growing collection of surgical tools, instruments and documents, it's full of stomach-turning things to look at.

319 THE INSECT ASYLUM

2870 N Milwaukee Avenue
Avondale ⑤
+1 312 961 7219
theinsectasylum.com

Bugs can be beautiful, especially when presented with care in a space this cute. Showcasing approximately 2500 specimens from its founder's collection, this store-front space draws curious passers-by to inspect insects on an intimate level.

320 LEATHER ARCHIVES & MUSEUM

6418 N Greenview Avenue
Rogers Park ⑥
+1 773 761 9200
leatherarchives.org

Caveat: This is not a museum devoted to animal hides. With a goal of normalizing leather, kink, BDSM and fetish through education, preservation, and community engagement, this nonprofit's collection is above and beyond the obvious accessories and costumes. One of the three original leather pride flags lives here, and there's a rich reading library.

5 *tiny* THEATERS

---

321 A RED ORCHID THEATRE

1531 N Wells St
Old Town ①
+1 312 943 8722
aredorchidtheatre.org

Award-winning acting and 30 years of productions justify the many accolades given to this ensemble and its intimate 70-seat theater. Serving the mission that "theatre is the greatest sustenance for the human spirit," A Red Orchid stages world premieres alongside classics reimagined. Oscar-nominated actor Michael Shannon is a founding member of the ensemble.

322 LIFELINE THEATRE

6912 N Glenwood Avenue
Rogers Park ⑥
+1 773 761 4477
lifelinetheatre.com

Situated in a beautiful old brick utility building, the 95-seat Lifeline Theatre has been a stalwart of independent theater since opening in 1982. With a mission of reimagining books and literary works to truly move audiences, the theater's production schedule sees a rotation of adaptations and a sprinkling of original works.

323 THE GIFT THEATRE

5344 W Lawrence
Avenue
Jefferson Park ⑥
+1 773 283 7071
thegifttheatre.org

Just 50 seats fit into this comfortable storefront theater where a minimal production schedule buys time to fine-tune the details. Originally conceived as a company to stage works as a 'gift' to underserved communities, the focus has since shifted to foster creative access to those who might not otherwise have it.

324 REDTWIST THEATRE

1044 W Bryn Mawr
Avenue
Edgewater ⑥
+1 773 728 7529
redtwisttheatre.org

When the audience's few dozen seats are worked into the set design itself, things get interesting. That's just part of the 'twist' with Redtwist, which has been staging intensely dramatic productions since its founding as a nonprofit in 2001. The company has won several locally coveted Jeff Awards for its creativity.

325 STEEP THEATRE

1044 W Berwyn
Avenue
Edgewater ⑥
+1 773 649 3186
steeptheatre.com

Staged in a former church with a dose of realness sometimes absent from theater productions, Steep uses its productions to explore the stories of everyday people in not-so-everyday scenarios. Founded in 2000 by three actors with virtually no budget, it's grown to a company of nearly 50 that's committed to spotlighting brand new and lesser-produced plays.

5 *places to*

LAUGH OUT LOUD

326 **COLE'S BAR**
2338 N Milwaukee Avenue
Logan Square [5]
+1 773 276 5802
colesbarchicago.com

Wednesdays are open-mic nights at this neighborhood bar, self-proclaimed as one of the best in the nation. The proof is in the performances: many locals who got their start testing out material at Cole's have since struck success as grand as *Saturday Night Live*. Bonus: open-mic night is free to attend.

326 COLE'S BAR

327 LOGAN SQUARE IMPROV

2825 W Diversey Avenue
Logan Square ⑤
+1 312 810 7450
logansquareimprov.com

This unassuming storefront is a delightfully cozy space to take in the city's up-and-coming comedic talent. Budget-priced shows run five nights a week and showcase students from the spot's improv classes as well as ringer improv troupes, stand-up comics working out their material, and more. BYOB.

328 THE NEO-FUTURIST THEATER

5153 N Ashland Avenue
Andersonville ⑥
+1 773 878 4557
neofuturists.org

As founders of *Too Much Light Makes the Baby Go Blind*, the longest-running show in town, the Neo-Futurists are in a class of their own. In this black box space, thousands of two-minute plays (aka 30 plays in 60 minutes) have been performed since the late 1980s.

329 BUGHOUSE THEATER

1910 W Irving Park Road
North Center ⑤
+1 773 998 1284
bughousetheater.com

Situated in an anonymous mixed-use building, this little nonprofit black-box comedy theater offers programming six nights of the week for affordable prices. Improv is the primary form of entertainment here, but variety shows blend stand-up and sketch comedy, and there are even a few musical comedy showcases.

330 THE COMEDY BAR

162 E Superior St
Magnificent Mile ①
+1 312 623 3532
comedybar.com

For a dinner-and-a-show experience, this polished club upstairs from Gino's East's Mag Mile location makes for a delicious night out. Stand-up acts take residency for a few nights of shows, and locals rotate into weekly tight-five showcases as well as a hosted talk show spinoff called the *The Late Nite Mic*.

5 places to catch
INDEPENDENT FILMS

---

331 MUSIC BOX THEATRE
  3733 N Southport
  Avenue
  Lakeview ⑤
  +1 773 871 6604
  musicboxtheatre.com

Opened in 1929 just in time to piggy-back on the golden age of cinema, the cavernous, 700-seat Music Box has maintained its character through the ups and downs of cinematic history. These days, a calendar of independent releases and cult classics are shown on both digital and 35-mm film, and a rotation of special series and festivals show year-round.

332 GENE SISKEL
  FILM CENTER
  164 N State St
  The Loop ②
  +1 312 846 2085
  siskelfilmcenter.org

Founded in the 1970s and renamed after the late beloved film critic, this comfortable theater is in the heart of the Loop's performance theater district. Independent films and classic revivals are just one part of its programming. In academic partnership with the School of the Art Institute, the film center hosts some 200 filmmaker appearances each year.

331 MUSIC BOX THEATRE

333 FACETS

1517 W Fullerton Avenue
Sheffield Neighbors [5]
+1 773 281 9075
facets.org

There's just one single-screen theater in this building, but as an institution, FACETS looms large. Established in 1975 as a nonprofit organization dedicated to the preservation of film, it's since grown to house a very small school, a very large video rental store, and a handful of camps, institutes and festivals, including the Chicago International Children's Film Festival.

334 DOC FILMS

1212 E 59th St, #3
Hyde Park [7]
+1 773 702 8574
docfilms.org

'Doc Films' is short for the University of Chicago's International House of Documentary Film Group. But in the near century since it was founded by a handful of students (it's the oldest student film society in the country), it's long expanded beyond documentaries. The group's 475-seat movie theater, the Max Palesky Cinema, underwent a major digital upgrade in 2023.

335 SWEET VOID CINEMA

3036 W Chicago Avenue, #1W
Humboldt Park [4]
+1 773 823 1283
sweetvoidcinema.com

This self-described microcinema is located in an anonymous brick building at the edge of Humboldt Park. Founded by a handful of local film students, who seek to support the city's ever-expanding community of filmmakers, Sweet Void hosts weekly workshops on screenwriting and spur-of-the-moment filmmaking, and also has produced a handful of its own films.

5 UNLIKELY
art destinations

336 ART ON THE MART FAÇADE

222 W Merchandise Mart Plaza, south façade
Riverwalk ②
artonthemart.com

When the sun goes down, the art comes up: projections from local and visiting artists are digitally on display for an hour or so, spanning the nearly 92.000 square feet of surface area of the building's façade. For viewing, the best seats are directly across the river on the Riverwalk Jetty, where speakers project any accompanying soundtrack.

337 CHICAGO RIVERWALK

Parallel to Wacker Drive from Lake St to the Lakefront Trail
Riverwalk ②
chicago.gov

Local artists were commissioned to brighten the empty spaces between retail along the Riverwalk and add color and character along the pedestrian trail. Among the most delightful is street artist Dont Fret's installation wrapping the western end. Dubbed *The People In Your Neighborhood*, it's a collection of 55 comic-like portraits of locals that define the artist's version of Chicago.

338 BIG CHICKS

5024 N Sheridan
Road
Uptown ⑥
+1 773 728 5511
bigchicks.com

It's easy to get distracted by the flirty crowd and hearty comfort food at this friendly LGBTQ haunt, but the walls reveal the spoils: an impressive collection of modern art by renowned local artists. From paintings by Lee Godie to photographs from Diane Arbus and Hollis Sigler, the common thread is simple: works by and about women.

339 O'HARE INTERNATIONAL AIRPORT MULTI-MODAL TERMINAL

10255 W Zemke
Boulevard
O'Hare ⑥
flychicago.com

O'Hare's brand-new rental car facility came with a 2,6-million-dollar art budget curated by iconic local artist and activist Theaster Gates. Among the pieces is *Palimpsest*, a gloriously colorful, large-scale tapestry by local multidisciplinary artist Nick Cave, most famous for his immaculately constructed 'soundsuits': wearable works of arts designed to emit sound while in motion.

340 VANDERPOEL ART MUSEUM

AT: RIDGE PARK
FIELDHOUSE
9625 S Longwood
Drive
Beverly
+1 773 294 8311
vanderpoelart
museum.org

Founded by friends and fans of a former teacher at the School of the Art Institute, this impressive collection of mostly paintings and drawings is crammed into a Chicago Parks Department building in Ridge Park. In all, there are around 600 works by 400 artists including Grant Wood, Mary Cassatt and others. Beyond exhibitions, the gallery hosts drawing classes.

5 inspiring
LIBRARIES

341 **CHICAGO PUBLIC LIBRARY WEST LOOP BRANCH**

122 N Aberdeen St
West Loop ④
+1 312 744 2995
chipublib.org

Designed by Skidmore, Owings & Merrill and opened in 2019, this smart adaptive-reuse project transformed a pair of Oprah Winfrey's former studios and offices into a stylish library. The building's original bow-truss ceiling is brightly lit, putting the lofty space on full display, and modern wood-and-black steel shelving emit cozy bookstore vibes.

342 **HAROLD WASHINGTON LIBRARY**

400 S State St
The Loop ②
+1 312 747 4300
chipublib.org

From its grand marble lobby to the ninth story's light-filled winter garden, the city's flagship library – the largest public library building in the world – is awe-inspiring. Each floor houses a dozen or so oak-trimmed study carrels and generous reading tables. Don't miss *Above and Beyond*, the sobering Vietnam War memorial installation featuring 58.307 personally stamped dog tags.

343 NEWBERRY LIBRARY
60 W Walton St
Gold Coast ①
+1 312 943 9090
newberry.org

In its present location since 1893, the regal Newberry is designed in a traditional Spanish Romanesque style, whose rich flairs and details are especially prominent in the beautiful foyer. The collection itself is rich in the humanities, and rotating exhibitions and frequent tours are open to the public.

344 RYERSON AND BURNHAM LIBRARIES
AT: ART INSTITUTE
OF CHICAGO
111 S Michigan
Avenue
The Loop ②
+1 312 443 3666
artic.edu/library

Beneath the museum's Grand Staircase are a pair of frosted paned-glass doors leading to this research respite, where archives from some of the city's most prominent architects live alongside remnants of the Chicago World's Fair of 1893. A curved ceiling, leaded-glass details, and robin egg blue paint outfit the skylit space; works from the museum's collection are displayed throughout.

345 POETRY FOUNDATION LIBRARY
61 W Superior St
River North ①
+1 312 787 7070
poetryfoundation.org

The only library in the Midwest dedicated to poetry, this is a special place. Housed in a sustainable, modernist building with a cleverly transparent black façade, the library evokes quietude from its pleasant garden to the blonde-wood shelving cataloguing some 30.000 volumes. Simple, modular seating areas are spread over the split-level space, flooded with natural light.

5 STREET ARTISTS

to spy

---

346 CODY HUDSON

Splitting time between Chicago and rural Wisconsin, Hudson has an unmistakably iconic style that's found its way into Nike campaigns and onto record covers, wrapped around beer cans and woven into blankets. You're likely to recognize his street and commercial art installations around town – the biggest of which is on the north side of 167 N Green Street.

347 DONT FRET

After a self-described unsuccessful stint in graffiti art, 'vaguely anonymous' street artist Dont Fret took to wheat-pasting his way across the city with lovably cartoonish depictions of local characters and buildings. Due to the nature of his preferred canvas – anonymous alleys and buildings earmarked for demolition – much of his work is fleeting. The exception is his installation on the Chicago Riverwalk.

348 JUSTUS ROE

The larger the scale, the smaller the detail. These seem to be the aesthetic parameters of Roe's colorful contributions, which are equally at home in upscale hotels as expressway underpasses. Works comprise fragments of geometry and wisps of color, blended in a whirlwind of activity. One prime example: 1001 S State Street.

349 CLS

Charles L. Schriver aka CLS is behind bursts of tidily arranged wood scraps nailed and tacked to construction sites and vacant buildings around town. Installations of raw and painted found scraps of plywood, casing and other throwaway whatnots are often updated over time as the artist revisits sites. Most are on the North Side, but he's installed as far as Hong Kong.

350 SICK FISHER

Buildings around town that have been given the Sick Fisher treatment stand out as if jumping from the pages of a comic book. Fisher typically covers entire storefronts (and interiors, and trucks, and buses, and bathroom floors) with hand-drawn repetition that lends them a whimsical, free-spirited quality. Check out the coach house on Hirsch Street just east of Maplewood Avenue.

SHEDD AQUARIUM

25 THINGS TO DO WITH CHILDREN

5 kid-friendly **MUSEUMS** and **INSTITUTIONS**

---

351 **ART INSTITUTE OF CHICAGO**

111 S Michigan Avenue
The Loop ②
+1 312 443 3600
artic.edu

Surprisingly approachable for the smallest patrons. Kids under 14 are free, and the maze of rooms and hallways mean there is plenty of stroller space and room to teeter around. Pint-sized favorites include the airy Modern Wing and the enthralling Thorne Miniature Rooms in the basement.

352 **HYDE PARK ART CENTER**

5020 S Cornell Avenue
Hyde Park ⑦
+1 773 324 5520
hydeparkart.org

This admission-free art center has a welcoming, no-nonsense approach. Rotating exhibitions showcase a range of engaging works – including an annual teen show – and the large installation spaces allow for room to stretch. The lovely cafe is a great respite for snack time and bathroom breaks.

353 **SHEDD AQUARIUM**

1200 S DuSable Lake Shore Drive
Museum Campus ③
+1 312 939 2438
sheddaquarium.org

With panoramic views of the lake, the Shedd opened in 1930 as one of the largest aquariums in the world, and today fosters a whopping 32.000 sea creatures. Don't miss the smiling beluga whales nor the playful sea otters, whose tiered-height tanks offer multiple viewpoints.

354 MUSEUM OF SCIENCE & INDUSTRY

5700 S DuSable Lake Shore Drive
Hyde Park ⑦
+1 773 684 1414
msichicago.org

Scale-model cities, a real submarine, flight simulators, a baby chick hatchery – there's a lot going on at the biggest science museum in the Western hemisphere. Permanent exhibits range from the art of the bicycle to the world's largest pinball machine, and seasonal programming means there's always something happening same-day.

355 THE FIELD MUSEUM

1400 S DuSable Lake Shore Drive
Museum Campus ③
+1 312 922 9410
fieldmuseum.org

This beautiful century-old museum is the home of one of Chicago's best known celebrities: Sue, the largest, most complete T-Rex skeleton in the world. Named for its discoverer, Sue is a must-see for budding archeologists and dino lovers. In roomy exhibits, all sorts of animals, plants, and other specimens of the natural world are displayed.

355 THE FIELD MUSEUM

5 OUTINGS

kids love

---

356 MAGGIE DALEY PARK

337 E Randolph St
New East Side ②
+1 312 742 3918
maggiedaleypark.com

A climbing structure, a skating ribbon, a miniature golf course, and a three-acre play garden are highlights of this massive park. Criss-crossed with a web of trails through rolling green spaces, it never feels too crowded despite its massive popularity on fair-weather days. The play garden alone features six different exploration areas demarcated for different ages.

357 GARFIELD PARK CONSERVATORY

300 N Central Park Avenue
Garfield Park (4)
+1 773 638 1766
garfieldconservatory.org

No matter the weather, it's always beautiful and balmy inside this gorgeous Victorian-era conservatory. Paved paths are stroller friendly, and the tickle of ferns on little noses is good for the soul. The Fern Room is a highlight with a trickling indoor lagoon, hungry koi fish and ever-present misting. Outside, beautiful gardens invite chasing butterflies.

358 PEGGY NOTEBAERT NATURE MUSEUM

2430 N Cannon Drive
Lincoln Park (5)
+1 773 755 5100
naturemuseum.org

Far from a traditional museum, this welcoming nature hub recently underwent a massive renovation to focus on play spaces for the tiniest botanists. The butterfly haven is a must-visit. A network of fun ramps and paths through prairie-lands and wetlands connect the building to the surrounding Lincoln Park.

359 'THE BEAN'

AT: MILLENNIUM PARK
201 E Randolph St
Millennium Park (2)
millenniumpark.org

Titled *Cloud Gate*, the city's famous 'bean', from renowned artist Anish Kapoor, is a natural magnet. Cool to the touch even on hot summer days, the sculpture's shiny metal tempts even the shyest kids to make silly faces, and exploring the underbelly of the bean is a trip.

360 LINCOLN PARK ZOO

2400 N Cannon Drive
Lincoln Park (5)
+1 312 742 2000
lpzoo.org

A pleasant and easy place to stroll for an hour or two. Founded in 1868 with a pair of swans gifted by New York's Central Park Zoo, there are now 1100 animals. Winding paths connect exhibits, and the beautiful Nature Boardwalk was designed by local starchitect Jeanne Gang.

5 SPLASH PADS

for hot summer days

361 CROWN FOUNTAIN

201 E Randolph St
Millennium Park ②
+1 312 742 1168
millenniumpark.org

Conceptual artist Jaume Plensa didn't exactly have dozens of barefooted children in mind while designing *Crown Fountain*, but this LED-powered human-gargoyle water feature belongs to them. Every five minutes, water spouts from the digital mouths of two 50-foot towers, filling a nearly flat reflecting pool, and splashes ensue.

362 PORTAGE PARK WATER PLAY AREA

4100 N Long Avenue
Portage Park ⑥
chicagoparkdistrict.com

The water play area in this vast North Side park is marked by a large, oval zero-depth pool, and an island of water features that draws kids like a magnet. Sprayers, pipes, wheels and a water slide come together for an action-packed hub for cooling off. The structure is covered, too, so there's a bit of shade.

361 **CROWN FOUNTAIN**

363 **ADAMS WATER SPRAY FEATURE**

1919 N Seminary Avenue
Ranch Triangle [5]
+1 312 742 7787
chicagoparkdistrict.com

This modest park's water playground is a popular draw. Simple, abstract interpretations of a sea dragon, a sailboat and a handful of curious looking blooms are the vessels for sprays of water. The tallest structure, resembling an abstract bell tower, features a large bucket that dramatically tips once it's full, to the delight of squealing kids below.

364 **MARY BARTELME PARK**

115 S Sangamon St
West Loop [4]
+1 312 746 5494
chicagoparkdistrict.com

From a distance, this modern park's simple, elegant collection of stainless steel gates look to be an abstract art installation, or an innovative way to light the path below. But come summer-time, these five gates emit a fine mist of water to the delight of neighborhood kids, providing just enough spray for a cooling effect.

365 **INDIAN BOUNDARY PARK**

2500 W Lunt Avenue
West Ridge [6]
+1 773 764 0338
chicagoparkdistrict.com

There's nothing fancy about this magnificent park's water play area, but it succeeds in its simplicity. A circular patio features a trio of plain red spray pipes accompanied by dancing bears, nodding to the Nature Play Center on the park's northwest side, and they're just the right height for kids to climb on their shoulders to cool off.

5 *delightful children's* SHOPS

366 **TIMELESS TOYS**
4749 N Lincoln Avenue
Lincoln Square [6]
+1 773 334 4445
timelesstoys.com

Opened in 1993 as an anchor for the neighborhood, this toy shop stocks wooden toys, classic games and truly timeless delights (puppets, puzzles, etc.) for children of all ages. Within the roomy storefront are sections devoted to playthings of all sorts, and a nice library at the back of the shop has all the greatest hits.

367 ***PLAY**
3109 W Logan Boulevard
Logan Square [5]
+1 773 227 6504
playtoysandbooks.com

Packed to the brim with all kinds of fun stuff for toddlers through tweens, this long-running neighborhood favorite is a common stop for kids' birthday parties thanks to its whimsical wrapping paper. Stuffies and books, painting supplies and dress-up, Lego and Brio – it's all here, carefully crammed into every nook and cranny of usable space.

368 PEACH FUZZ

1005 N California
Avenue
West Town ④
+1 312 881 9971
littlepeachfuzz.com

This playfully pastel shop with thoughtful details (curious little ones will love discovering the secret nook) is a dream come true for parents looking for pretty yet practical finds. Inclusiveness of all stripes is a running theme, and there are occasionally kids' playtime events in the sweet little backyard.

369 KIDO

1137 S Delano Court
South Loop ②
+1 312 285 2957
kidochicago.com

Kido bills itself as a diverse kids boutique, prioritizing representation and inclusivity across families of all shapes, sizes, colors and traditions. That rings especially true in this welcoming shop's impressive library, overflowing with must-reads recommended by educators and artists in the know. A charming collection of sustainable toys and sweet, comfy clothing round out the wares.

370 TOYS ET CETERA

1502 E 55th St
Hyde Park ⑦
+1 773 324 6039
toysetcetera.com

This long-running Hyde Park toy shop with confetti-patterned carpet carries more than 10.000 toys in its roomy storefront. There's always been an emphasis on educational and STEM-centric toys (even before STEM was a thing), and the incredibly well organized shelves – and helpful staff – make shopping fun.

5 kid-friendly
RESTAURANTS

371 GATHER

4539 N Lincoln
Avenue
Lincoln Square ⑥
+1 773 506 9300
gatherchicago.com

Sundays are family nights at this popular go-to: family-style portions are doled out at your table's pace, and kids eat free. There's a salad for the table, seasonal roasted veg, a bowl of the delicious housemade fusilli, a main protein everyone can agree on, and a yummy, sticky brown butter cake to end things on a sweet note.

372 PARSON'S CHICKEN & FISH

5721 N Clark St
Andersonville ⑥
+1 773 654 1141
parsonschicken
andfish.com

Popular among neighborhood hipsters and young families alike, Parson's makes it easy to please a group. From crispy fried chicken and battered fish sticks to yummy hushpuppies, there are plenty of kid-friendly options. Bleacher-style seating and generous patios give wee ones free range to roam while parents sip Negroni Slushies.

373 COMMUNITY TAVERN

4038 N Milwaukee Avenue
Portage Park [6]
+1 773 283 6080
communitytavern.com

This extra-friendly neighborhood restaurant is just as popular for parents' nights out as boisterous family dinners with little ones. Kids eat free Tuesday through Thursday, as well as Sunday nights, and the dedicated kids menu means grownups can indulge in Korean-inspired Kim-Cheese Fries, dumplings, and bibimbap while pickier eaters enjoy burgers and grilled cheese.

374 HONEY BUTTER FRIED CHICKEN

3361 N Elston Avenue
Avondale [5]
+1 773 478 4000
honeybutter.com

Deliciously crispy fried chicken and bite-sized honey butter-kissed cornbread are the calling cards at this cozy Avondale joint. With servings ranging from 8-piece down to the children's 'Mini Meal', the menu is full of parent-pleasing sides (pimento mac'n cheese, rosemary-schmaltzed smashed potatoes), and the generous patio and magnetic board in the back are kid-friendly.

375 THE STOPALONG

1812 N Milwaukee Avenue
Bucktown [5]
+1 773 394 4694
thestopalong.com

Cheery yellow awnings and throwback vibes appeal to 'the kid in all of us', but it's especially great for little kids with ticking time-bomb tummies. Flip a coin to choose between the juicy smashburger or the chewy, bready pizza, and save room for froyo and cookies. The food comes out pretty fast, but arcade games help pass the time.

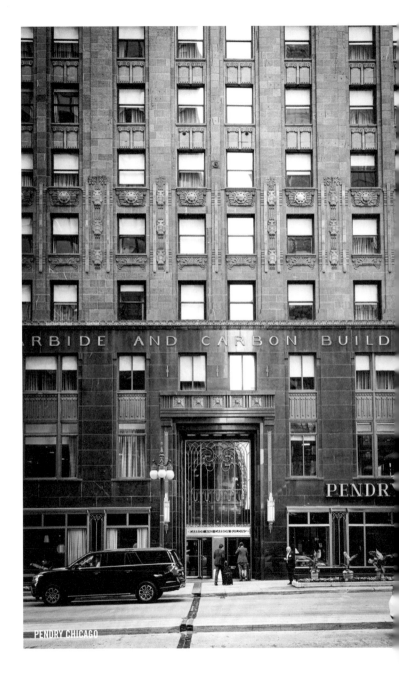

45 PLACES
TO SLEEP

---

5 **HIP** *hotels*

376 **THE HOXTON**

The local outpost of this British hotel features a plush, livingroom-like lobby that buzzes with energy. Featuring an eclectic collection of art by locals, there's a relaxed, lived-in feel that mimics its crowd's artful taste. Rooms are comfortably appointed, and a duo of very good restaurants invite lingering.

377 **FREEHAND CHICAGO**

A go-to for free-spirited guests: an eclectic, bohemian-styled lobby, a cocktail bar whose reputation preceded its opening, and guest rooms that feature clever design details and tactile, textured nuances. The restored 1927 building complements the allure of a nomadic lifestyle with comfort and charisma, and feels at home in the heart of its bustling nightlife-centric neighborhood.

378 **THE ROBEY**

Sitting pretty in the very heart of lively Wicker Park, the Robey's art deco flatiron building sticks out from the area's skyline in the best possible way. Common spaces are handsome and inviting, finished in dark wood paneling, moody jewel tones, marble and oil-rubbed bronze hardware.

379 SOPHY HYDE PARK

1411 E 53rd St
Hyde Park ⑦
+1 773 289 1003
sophyhotel.com

This neighborhood newcomer fills a void in South Side accommodations. Sophy is situated in a new construction building that marries the neighborhood's architectural history with modern design. Rooms feature hardwood floors layered with geometric area rugs, and bold large-format works of art decorate the walls.

380 SOHO HOUSE CHICAGO

113-125 N Green St
West Loop ④
+1 312 521 8000
sohohousechicago.com

Chicago's outpost of the international members club beckons with stylishly timeless bedrooms. A rooftop pool provides the backdrop for people watching over cocktails, and guests have access to the extraordinary gym and Cowshed spa. Look for original artwork on property from local greats Kerry James Marshall and Theaster Gates.

379 SOPHY HYDE PARK

5 UNIQUE
places to stay

381 INN AT LONGMAN & EAGLE

2657 N Kedzie
Avenue
Logan Square ⑤
+1 773 276 7110
longmanandeagle.com/
sleep

With just a half-dozen rooms above this hip gastropub, this is an inn in the truest sense of the term. Historic features and modern amenities mix in exposed-brick bedrooms accented with local art. Each room has a cassette player and mixtapes, and drink tokens can be cashed in for drams of whiskey at the bar.

382 THE PUBLISHING HOUSE B&B

108 N May St
West Loop ④
+1 312 554 5857
publishinghouse
bnb.com

A 1909 former printing house whose sunlit windows and high ceilings make a welcoming home-away-from-home for modern tourists. Each room is furnished with a pleasing blend of antiques and modern pieces, and the large common areas – living and dining with a split fireplace; a roomy kitchen – invite lingering. Downstairs, the owners' wine bar draws locals for date nights.

383 THE WHEELER MANSION

2020 S Calumet
Avenue
Prairie District ③
+1 312 945 2020
thewheelermansion.com

Built in the grand Second Empire style, this mansion just off "Millionaire's Row" has been restored to its original grandeur for luxury guests. Each of the 11 rooms is unique, and all have access to the ornate common spaces and lush garden, where afternoon croquet and ping pong are popular. Brunch is a posh affair with live music.

384 THE GUESTHOUSE HOTEL

4872 N Clark St
Uptown ⑥
+1 773 564 9568
theguesthousehotel.com

The Guesthouse is a collection of one-, two-, and three-bedroom suites in a shared condominium building, accented with the personal touches of a hotel staff. Situated just south of the hubbub of Andersonville, the modern building is within walking distance of one of the city's most beloved neighborhoods, with tried-and-true dining, drinking, and diverse culture.

385 WICKER PARK INN

1331 N Wicker
Park Avenue
Wicker Park ④
+1 773 486 2743
wickerparkinn.com

On a quiet side street in this walkable, tree-lined neighborhood, this historic row house is divided into nine modest bedrooms with en suite baths. Exposed bricks and working fireplaces (in some rooms) lend a homey feel, skylights in the second floor add a fresh perspective, and the sunny kitchen hosts daily continental breakfast.

5 **LUXE** *hotels*

386 **THE LANGHAM CHICAGO**

330 N Wabash Avenue
River North ⓘ
+1 312 923 9988
langhamhotels.com/chicago

Located in Mies van der Rohe's landmark IBM building, the Langham sits in the center of the Chicago River's main branch with stunning 180-degree views. Luxe, freshly styled rooms feature modern craft furniture with soothing curves. With a nod to Mies, the hotel is decorated with artwork inspired by the Bauhaus movement.

387 **THE PENINSULA CHICAGO HOTEL**

108 E Superior St
Magnificent Mile ⓘ
+1 312 337 2888
peninsula.com/chicago

The pinnacle of luxury, from its cavernous communal spaces to its multi-story spa and pool complex towering above Michigan Avenue. Rooms are divinely appointed in a welcoming traditional style with jaw-dropping views and spa-like bathrooms. Plan to dine at least once in The Lobby, the hotel's all-day dining room with floor-to-ceiling views of the terrace.

388 PENDRY CHICAGO

230 N Michigan
Avenue
The Loop ②
+1 312 777 9000
pendrychicago.com

Some say this building was designed to look like a champagne bottle: dark green and gold terra cotta are topped by a 24-karat gold-leaf cap. Plenty of the stuff flows in this opulently outfitted hotel, where design choices complement the building's art deco glam. The 24th-floor rooftop terrace serves jaw-dropping views and lots of rosé.

389 PARK HYATT CHICAGO

800 N Michigan
Avenue
Magnificent Mile ①
+1 312 335 1234
hyatt.com/chicago

A Magnificent Mile icon since opening in 1980 as the first Park Hyatt in the world. A 2022 glow-up refreshed the property to the tune of 60 million dollars, and fortunately maintained its long-running restaurant, NoMI. With floor-to-ceiling cantilevered windows facing the lake, the seventh-floor dining room boasts incredible views.

390 NOBU HOTEL CHICAGO

155 N Peoria St
West Loop ④
+1 312 779 8888
chicago.nobuhotels.com

Behind the plain-jane street entrance lies a luxuriously minimalist lobby with two striking features: an oversized kintsugi sculpture centered on the wall, and the hotel's alluring fragrance – lemongrass-ginger. The beautifully simple Japanese-inspired decor extends to the signature restaurant, connected to the hotel via a subterranean passageway. Further underground are the hotel spa and tranquillity pool.

5 BOUTIQUE *hotels*

391 HOTEL ZACHARY

3630 N Clark St
Wrigleyville ⑤
+1 773 302 2300
hotelzachary.com

Baseball fans aren't the only ones who can appreciate this handsome hotel within home run distance of Wrigley Field. Spanning seven floors with box-seat views of the ballpark, it's finished in a vintage clubhouse feel with leather details, brass fixtures, and ivy-green accents. Outposts of some of the city's most popular foodie spots are just downstairs.

392 21C MUSEUM HOTEL CHICAGO

55 E Ontario St
River North ①
+1 312 660 6100
21cchicago.com

As the northernmost outpost of the 21c group of museum-hotels, Chicago's location features this mini-chain's knack for marrying curious visual arts installations with modern, comfortable rooms and suites. Renowned local artists are invited to take over the walls throughout the year, and lecture and performance series are sprinkled into the calendar.

393 THOMPSON CHICAGO

21 E Bellevue Place
Gold Coast ①
+1 312 266 2100
thompsonchicago.com

Tucked off of pedestrian-heavy Viagra Triangle, this chic boutique hotel is subtly stylish and exceptionally comfortable. Upper-floor rooms offer glimpses of the lake, and the ground floor lobby leads to an inviting bar. It's located within walking distance of high-end shopping and loads of dining options.

394 VICEROY CHICAGO

1118 N State St
Gold Coast ①
+1 312 586 2000
viceroyhotelsand
resorts.com/chicago

When the hotel was developed in 2018, only the façade of the original 1920s Cedar Hotel was spared, and an ultra-modern accordion-like glass tower was built behind it. The result: the amenities of brand-new architecture with a distinctive front door, and plenty of cubist-influenced style inside. The rooftop pool and lounge, Devereaux, is a fabulous perk.

395 VIRGIN HOTELS CHICAGO

203 N Wabash
Avenue
The Loop ②
+1 312 940 4400
virginhotels.com/
chicago

There's something about a red carpet that makes an entrance unforgettable. Chicago's location of this British chain dons the brand's signature red in spades, from its lofty lobby bar sparkling with a spray of suspended light bulbs, to the intimately rooftop lounge, Cerise, with dazzling views of the skyline.

5 handsome
HISTORIC *hotels*

396 **CHICAGO ATHLETIC ASSOCIATION**

12 S Michigan
Avenue
The Loop ②
+1 312 940 3552
chicagoathletic
hotel.com

Opened in 1893 as a men's club, the Chicago Athletic Association underwent a transformative renovation in 2015 – and finally opened to the public. Carefully preserved reminders from yesteryear shine in every corner, like the vintage mailboxes tucked beneath the grand marble stairway. Athletics still play a role: the hotel's Game Room features a bocce court, table shuffleboard and more.

397 **THE DRAKE**

140 E Walton Place
Magnificent Mile ①
+1 312 787 2200
thedrakehotel.com

Completed in 1920 by the same architects as the Palmer House, The Drake has maintained its stately Italian Renaissance style for more than a century. Subtle updates here and there lend the illusion that the hotel is seemingly frozen in time, and long-standing traditions – like afternoon tea in the luxe Palm Court and cocktails at Coq d'Or – feel truly special.

398 STAYPINEAPPLE, AN ICONIC HOTEL

1 W Washington St
The Loop ②
+1 312 940 7997
staypineapple.com/
chicago

Located in the historic Reliance Building skyscraper completed in 1895, this hip hotel manages to make bright, modern comforts feel right at home alongside stunning century-old iron elevator banks and stairwells. Be sure to enjoy at least one meal in Atwood, the lovely cafe named after the building's final architect.

399 LONDONHOUSE CHICAGO

85 E Wacker Drive
The Loop ②
+1 312 357 1200
londonhouse
chicago.com

This stunning 1923 neoclassical skyscraper shines with true Jazz Age sparkle. Enter through the original lobby to experience the grandeur of a gorgeous vaulted rotunda. Opulent elevator banks lead guests to the second story lobby bar, and the primary reason locals flock here in the summer: LondonHouse Rooftop lounge, with arguably the best views of the city.

400 MILLENNIUM KNICKERBOCKER HOTEL

163 E Walton Place
Magnificent Mile ①
+1 312 751 8100
knickerbocker
hotel.com

Opened in the shadow of The Drake hotel in 1927, the original hotel located in this Gothic Revival building was destined for a series of historic tenants. Presidents and gangsters walked its halls, and Hugh Hefner rebranded the building as the Playboy Hotel for a time in the 1970s. Vintage details like the stunning Crystal Ballroom still shine.

5 hotels with
INCREDIBLE VIEWS

401 **HOTEL LINCOLN**
1816 N Clark St
Lincoln Park [5]
+1 312 254 4700
hotellincoln chicago.com

What this boutique hotel lacks in height, it makes up for in depth of color. Perched directly on sprawling Lincoln Park, Hotel Lincoln's modest 12 stories offer a front-row view during all four seasons of the park's transitions, and North Avenue Beach beyond. Grab drinks at the J. Parker Rooftop bar to take it all in.

402 RADISSON BLU AQUA HOTEL

221 N Columbus
Drive
New East Side ②
+1 312 638 6686
radissonblu
chicago.com

Located in architect Jeanne Gang's stunning Aqua Tower in one of the eastern-most neighborhoods off the Loop, the Radisson Blu captures peerless views of Lake Michigan to the east and densely dramatic city views to the west. Hand-somely outfitted common areas and a decent restaurant anchor the hotel.

403 WALDORF ASTORIA CHICAGO

11 E Walton St
Gold Coast ①
+1 312 646 1300
waldorfastoria
chicagohotel.com

In the heart of the Gold Coast with matchless views of the city and the lake, this 60-story tower is anchored by a courtyard designed in a grand Parisian style, complete with heated pavers for luxurious winter wayfinding. While there, pop into Bernard's, the jewelbox of a cocktail bar on the second floor.

404 TRUMP INTERNATIONAL HOTEL & TOWER

401 N Wabash
Avenue
River North ①
+1 312 588 8000
trumphotels.com/
chicago

Second in height only to the Sears (Willis) Tower, this tower sits in an ideal location with vantages both tall and wide. Follow the pleasant pedestrian path from Michigan Avenue, then take the elevator to Terrace 16 where the upscale restaurant offers a wide-angle view of the skyline. Rebar, on the mezzanine level, features wall-to-wall views of the River.

405 FOUR SEASONS HOTEL CHICAGO

120 E Delaware Place
Magnificent Mile ①
+1 312 280 8800
fourseasons.com/
chicago

One of the few hotels tall enough to offer unobscured views of the Lake Michigan horizon as well as the jagged skyline. Book drinks at the Mile High Cocktail Club on the 46th floor: a fun tribute to the golden age of air travel.

5 hotels with great
LOBBY BARS

---

406 CIRA
AT: THE HOXTON
200 N Green St
Fulton Market ④
+1 312 761 1777
cirachicago.com

Though technically a full-service restaurant, Cira's footprint is so large, there are plenty of pockets for everything from coffee dates to solo scrolling by the always-roaring fire. By day, comfortable couches and a welcoming, naturally lit bar welcome leisurely lunches, and the local after-work crowd moves in for happy hour as the lights dim.

407 THE LIBRARY
AT: AMBASSADOR CHICAGO
1301 N State Parkway
Gold Coast ①
+1 312 787 3700
ambassadorchicago.com

The size of this little coffee/cocktail bar lends it an intimate feel that's immediately cozy. With eye-catching portraits on the walls, leather chairs facing a custom limestone fireplace, and low-slung couches and coffee tables stacked with art monographs, it's as comfortable as a posh friend's reading room.

408 SALONE NICO

AT: THOMPSON HOTEL
21 E Bellevue Place
Gold Coast ①
+1 312 994 7100
nicoosteria.com

A welcome respite from buzzy Rush Street, this understated lobby bar is a quiet and comfortable location for a solo glass of wine or a shared bottle and bites. Though the hotel's check-in desk is nearby, a fireplace and club chairs break up the room, creating space to spread out.

409 DRAWING ROOM

AT: CHICAGO ATHLETIC ASSOCIATION
12 S Michigan Avenue
The Loop ②
+1 312 792 3536
lsdatcaa.com/
drawing-room

With tall ceilings, dark lighting and handsome leather, the aptly named Drawing Room is a comfortable gathering place for comings and goings of locals and travelers alike. Library tables, cozy nooks, and fireside leather couches are all up for grabs, and unobtrusive staff regularly make the rounds offering beverages and bites, if you're hungry.

410 BROKEN SHAKER

AT: FREEHAND HOTEL
19 E Ohio St
River North ①
+1 312 940 3699
brokenshaker.com

Fuzzy wall hangings, a red brick fireplace, retro totems and yellow table-lamp lighting lend this famous cocktail spot a kitschy vibe that's ideal for killing a few hours. Banquette seating is mixed with low-slung couches and side tables for a range of seating options, and a recently added all-day menu means you'll never go hungry.

THE LIBRARY AT AMBASSADOR CHICAGO

409 DRAWING ROOM AT CHICAGO ATHLETIC ASSOCIATION

5 hotels that
FEEL LIKE AN ESCAPE

---

411 **KIMPTON GRAY HOTEL**

122 W Monroe St
The Loop ②
+1 312 750 9012
grayhotelchicago.com

The scale of this stately hotel in a handsome, historic building makes the outside world disappear. Named for the luxe Georgia Gray marble that lines the foyers and grand staircase, its sophisticated rooms soar above the financial heart of the city. Have a cocktail in the library-themed bar inspired by a set of encyclopedias uncovered during renovation.

412 **SABLE AT NAVY PIER**

900 E Grand Avenue
Navy Pier ①
+1 872 710 5700
sablehotel.com

Navy Pier is notoriously overrun with tourists, but Sable feels like a private cruise ship parked in safe harbors. The seafaring-inspired upscale hotel features peerless views of Lake Michigan and the skyline, and some of the most beautiful lakeside dining experiences in the city. Its rooftop lounge, Offshore, is the largest in the country.

413 AMBASSADOR HOTEL

1301 N State Parkway
Gold Coast [1]
+1 312 787 3700
ambassador chicago.com

Tucked onto a side street in a quiet residential area known for lap dogs and tony mansions, the Ambassador could easily be mistaken for a well-appointed doorman building. Opened in the height of Hollywood's golden age, it was regularly frequented by celebrities, including Marilyn Monroe, Frank Sinatra and Humphrey Bogart, looking to hide away from the spotlight of the Magnificent Mile.

414 THE HOTEL AT MIDTOWN

2444 N Elston Avenue
Bucktown [5]
+1 773 687 7600
midtownhotel chicago.com

To truly get away from it all, book a stay at this luxe athletic club hotel with amenities for miles...which sits miles away from the downtown action. Minimalist, modern rooms – leather chairs, muted colored room murals, spa-like bathrooms – set the mood for serious relaxation after a full day of athleisure, even if you're just in it for the spa.

415 HOTEL VERSEY

644 W Diversey Parkway
Lakeview [5]
+1 773 525 7010
hotelversey.com

Camouflaged by the busy Clark and Broadway intersection, this affordable hotel promotes guests to 'stay like a local'. Situated in the middle of a bustling retail and residential neighborhood, it's a far cry from the tourist-heavy main drag. With favorite music venues, movie theaters, and casual cafes close by, it's easy to blend into the crowd.

5 big, **FLASHY** hotels

416 THE BLACKSTONE

636 S Michigan
Avenue
South Loop ②
+1 312 447 0955
theblackstonehotel.com

Set in a grand Victorian building with
all the trimmings, this luxury landmark
hotel is famous for hosting presidents and
celebrities. Inspired by early-1900s French
architecture, its polished marble interiors
are accented with gilded, neoclassical
beaux-arts flourishes, lending a grand and
important air to virtually every room.
Modern works from local artists keeps
things current.

416 THE BLACKSTONE

417 THE RITZ-CARLTON, CHICAGO

160 E Pearson St
Magnificent Mile ①
+1 312 266 1000
ritzcarltonchicago.com

Tucked just off of Michigan Avenue inside a tastefully simple, bellhop-flanked entrance is the city's Ritz-Carlton. Take the elevators to the 12th-floor lobby: the newly refreshed, decidedly modern space offers a teaser of the soaring views.

418 HYATT REGENCY CHICAGO

151 E Wacker Drive
The Loop ②
+1 312 565 1234
hyattregency
chicago.com

The city's largest hotel by far, existing on a Vegas-like scale. More than 2000 generously large rooms are scattered throughout its twin towers' 228.000 square feet, which include several dining options, common spaces for meeting and lounging, and amenities including a game room.

419 INTERCONTINENTAL CHICAGO MAGNIFICENT MILE

505 N Michigan
Avenue
Magnificent Mile ①
+1 312 944 4100
intercontinental
chicago.com

The roaring twenties are alive and well at this beautifully revived hotel. Home to the largest crystal chandelier in the country and a swimming pool to die for, the building has undergone a series of expensive and extensive rehabs including mural restorations completed by an art historian that previously worked on the Sistine Chapel.

420 PALMER HOUSE HILTON

17 E Monroe St
The Loop ②
+1 312 726 7500
palmerhousehilton
hotel.com

The present-day Palmer House is the third version of Victorian-era developer Potter Palmer's dream hotel, which became more opulent with each rebuild. This dazzling building with many art deco-era details hosts more than 1600 guest rooms.

PROMONTORY POINT

40 WEEKEND ACTIVITIES

———

5 neighborhood
FARMERS MARKETS

421 **LOGAN SQUARE FARMERS MARKET**
Logan Boulevard between Kedzie Avenue and Whipple St
Logan Square ⑤
+1 773 489 3222
logansquarefarmer smarket.org

Absorbing space over three wide city blocks during the warm-weather months, this is one of the largest farmers markets in the city. More than 40 vendors create one continuous, wide aisle of greengrocers, European-inspired stinky-cheese paninis, hyper-local provisions, and more. There's live music nearly every day of the market, too.

422 **GREEN CITY MARKET**
1817 N Clark St
Lincoln Park ⑤
+1 773 217 0776
greencitymarket.org

Founded in 1999 as a nonprofit to raise awareness about food education, Green City has been named one of the best sustainable markets in the country. From April through October, the massive market operates in three locations: on the lawn in Lincoln Park, in the West Loop, and a smaller market in Avondale, where it moves in colder months.

423 DALEY PLAZA CITY MARKET

50 W Washington St
The Loop ②

On Thursdays from May to October, in the shadow of the Picasso statue, this central square comes alive with the city's longest running public market. It draws primarily greengrocers and a handful of baked goods vendors, and there's usually at least one flower stand adding a punch of color into the mix.

424 LINCOLN SQUARE FARMERS MARKET

N Lincoln and
W Leland Avenues
Lincoln Square ⑥
+1 872 806 0685
*lincolnsquare.org/
farmers-market*

Crammed into the little plaza adjacent to the Western Brown Line stop, this modest market draws around 40 vendors, from regional farms to local provisions. Beyond the stalls of vegetables, fruits and artisanal breads, there are a handful of prepared foods makers, too. This Tuesday/Thursday market runs through the end of November.

425 SOUTH LOOP FARMERS MARKET

AT: PRINTERS ROW PARK
632 S Dearborn St
Printers Row ②
+1 312 401 2688
*southloopfarmers
market.com*

Opposite the elegant 1880s-era Dearborn Station in Printers Row, around 50 vendors set up around a decorative fountain to sell everything from craft cocktails to handcrafted dog apparel. (Plenty of vendors peddle greens, cheeses and preserves, too.) It runs on Saturdays from May through October; a second market is open in Grant Park on Thursdays.

5 places to go DANCING

426 **SLIPPERY SLOPE**
2357 N Milwaukee Avenue
Logan Square [5]
+1 773 799 8504
slipperyslope chicago.com

Bottle service and velvet ropes would likely be laughed off by the casual, carefree crowds at this incredibly popular late-night DJ bar. Open only on the weekends (Thursday, Friday and Saturday nights), there's no cover, no reservations, and no pretence. Festively lit with a red glow and upbeat tunes, Slippery Slope is always a good time.

427 **PODLASIE CLUB**
2918 N Central Park Avenue
Avondale [5]
+1 773 276 0841
podlasiechicago.com

This old-school Polish bar started heating up a few years ago when a handful of young creatives began hosting monthly dance parties dubbed the Podlasie Pleasure Club. Now fully revived, Podlasie hosts a mix of long-established and emerging DJs most nights of the week, spinning everything from techno-house to early 2000s UK dubstep.

426 SLIPPERY SLOPE

428 BEAUTY BAR CHICAGO

1444 W Chicago Avenue
Noble Square [4]
linktr.ee/beautybarchicago

Opened in 2010 with a retro beauty-bar theme (think hair-dryer sets and manicure stations), Beauty Bar remains a go-to for laidback dance parties with throwback themes like '90s Night, Emo vs. Pop Punk, and Y2K. There's often no cover at the medium-sized venue, and the crowd is one of the friendliest in town.

429 SMARTBAR

3730 N Clark St
Lakeview [5]
smartbarchicago.com

Top DJs from all over the country regularly stop in to this stalwart of the city's nightlife scene. Most nights are billed as shows rather than parties, with set start times, advanced ticket sales, and day-of-show covers. With a relatively small dancefloor, the vibe gets strong as the night goes on.

430 BERLIN

954 W Belmont Avenue
Lakeview [5]
+1 773 348 4975
berlinchicago.com

Celebrating 40 years of LGBTQ-friendly dance parties, Berlin is the city's most famous dance club. It regularly wins awards for both Best Gay Bar and Best Non-Gay Bar – which is to say, anyone and everyone is welcome. Drag shows are peppered into the calendar alongside disco nights, industry nights, and a standing late-night blend that runs most Saturdays until dawn.

5 DAY TRIPS

431 INDIANA DUNES, INDIANA

1215 N State Road 49
Porter, Indiana
+1 219 926 2255
indianadunes.com

Just an hour outside of the city, the Dunes are a soothing, sandy nature fix. The Indiana Dunes National Park stretches 20 miles (32 kilometers) along the southern shore of Lake Michigan with protected wildlife areas rich with flora and fauna, though most of the dunes are quite literally sand. Features 45 miles (72,5 kilometers) of hiking, horse and bike trails.

432 NEW BUFFALO, MICHIGAN

newbuffalo.com

Just one in a string of little southwest Michigan lakeside towns known as Harbor Country, this hamlet of less than 2000 people is a popular destination for a quick beach-town getaway. Less than 90 minutes from the city, it's home to antique shops, art galleries, waterfront boutique hotels, and wineries open for tours.

433 LAKE GENEVA, WISCONSIN

+1 262 248 4416
visitlakegeneva.com

Located less than two hours from downtown, this lake community is a wonderful, walkable place to wile away an afternoon. Ice-cream shops and antiques line the main streets leading to the historic Riviera Marina building, but there are a few surprises here, too, including the Dungeon Hobby Shop Museum: the birthplace of Dungeons & Dragons.

434 GALENA, ILLINOIS

+1 815 776 9200
visitgalena.org

Walking down Main Street here feels like stepping back in time. Nearly the entire town has been designated a historic district, preserving its quaint 1840s red-brick buildings. Ulysses S. Grant's home – a gift from upon his victorious return from the Civil War – is one of many buildings open for tours, and local eateries, galleries and shops fill the spaces between.

435 STARVED ROCK STATE PARK, ILLINOIS

Oglesby, Illinois
+1 815 667 4726
*dnr.illinois.gov/parks/
park.starvedrock.html*

Two hours from downtown Chicago, this vast park invites visitors to chase waterfalls, traverse wooden bridges and explore its 18 moss-covered canyons. A tree canopy made up of red oaks, white pines, cedars, maples and hickories provides shade for hiking the more than 13 miles (21 kilometers) of trails, and come fall, it's a stunning show of foliage.

5 places to catch great
LOCAL BANDS

436 THALIA HALL

1807 S Allport St
Pilsen
+1 312 526 3851
thaliahallchicago.com

Established as a multi-purpose public house way back in 1892, this show-stopping historic building is now Thalia Hall: a hauntingly beautiful space in which to see local and nationally touring acts. Genres span from indie folk to experimental jazz, and the roomy upstairs balcony has the best views.

437 SCHUBAS TAVERN

3159 N Southport Avenue
Lakeview [5]
+1 773 525 2508
lh-st.com

Situated in a former Schlitz tied house, Schubas has hosted locals and touring acts since opening in 1989, and with a capacity of just 150 people or so, its cozy back room remains one of the most intimate places in the city to experience live music. Up front, the historic bar serves a nice variety of tap beers.

438 EMPTY BOTTLE

1035 N Western Avenue
Ukrainian Village [4]
+1 773 276 3600
emptybottle.com

A relic from the early 1990s, this beloved bar has hosted some of the world's most respected and notable acts on their way to breaking big. Free Monday night shows are a great way to get a sense for the local scene, and breakout touring acts tend to fill the rest of the week.

439 HIDEOUT
1354 W Wabansia Avenue
Clybourn Corridor [5]
+1 773 227 4433
hideoutchicago.com

A Chicago original. For nearly 30 years, the space has hosted live music and programming, and is the go-to venue to take in emerging singer-songwriters, alternative bands, and honky tonk jams in the front room. The small wood-paneled back room features a small stage, an old upright piano, and a chequered linoleum floor scuffed from decades of dancing.

440 SLEEPING VILLAGE
3734 W Belmont Avenue
Avondale [5]
+1 773 654 3971
sleeping-village.com

This post-modern bar and music room has earned a loyal following since opening in 2018. Local indie rock and folk acts are peppered into the mix of nationally touring bands, opening shows as well as carrying them on their own. The state-of-the-art music room is separate from the comfortable main bar, so there's room to converse and socialize.

438 EMPTY BOTTLE

5 *perfect* PICNIC *spots*

441 **WICKER PARK FOUNTAIN**
1425 N Damen Avenue
Wicker Park 4
+1 312 742 7529
chicagoparkdistrict.com

Surrounded by coffee shops, taco joints and slices to go, this popular public park and its charming fountain are perfect for a casual bite in the sunshine. For prime people watching, nab a bench facing the fountain or bring a blanket to spread on the shady grassy area.

442 **LINCOLN PARK GRANDMOTHER'S GARDEN**
N Stockton Drive and Webster Avenue
Lincoln Park 5
chicagoparkdistrict.com

This beautifully landscaped and immaculately maintained garden encompasses a large swath of land directly south of the Lincoln Park Conservatory. Grab some sushi or a cup of frozen yogurt along nearby Clark Street, then find a sunny spot on the lawn with a view of the charming Goose and Angels fountain.

443 JAPANESE GARDEN AT JACKSON PARK

6300 S Cornell
Avenue
Jackson Park ⑦
+1 773 256 0903
gardenofthe
phoenix.com

Especially in early spring with the cherry blossoms in bloom, this is a peaceful and beautiful spot to stop. This little garden and its larger location, on Jackson Park's vast Wooded Island, are remnants from the Chicago World's Fair of 1893. A mile west on 57th Street, the University of Chicago's commercial district has options for light bites.

444 HUMBOLDT PARK BOATHOUSE

1301 N Humboldt
Drive
Humboldt Park ④
+1 312 742 7549
chicagoparkdistrict.com

With 200 acres of prairies, meadows, nature vistas and more, Humboldt Park is one of the largest parks on the North Side. All paths lead to the Boathouse in the center of the park overlooking a pleasant lagoon. Street vendors sell Puerto Rican snacks, and during the warm months, swan-shaped pedal boats are for rent.

445 GREAT LAWN AT MILLENNIUM PARK

201 E Randolph St
Millennium Park ②
+1 312 742 1168
millenniumpark.org

A state-of-the-art sound system and genius quick-dry drainage system make this green patch adjacent to Pritzker Pavilion one of the poshest lawns in the city. During summer evenings, the Frank Gehry-designed bandshell hosts free concerts, and the city flocks with picnic baskets to enjoy the twilight soundtrack.

443 JAPANESE GARDEN AT JACKSON PARK

5 **SWIMMING** *spots*

---

446 **IDA CROWN NATATORIUM**

1330 W Chicago
Avenue
West Town ④
+1 312 746 5490
chicagoparkdistrict.com

In an otherwise run-of-the-mill public
park on a busy avenue, this wonderfully
whimsical mid-century enclosed
swimming structure begs for attention.
Square glass windows in a sprinkle of
primary colors allow a generous amount
of natural light into the natatorium,
where the colored windows playfully
reflect against the water. The pool is open
to the public.

447 **INTERCONTINENTAL HOTEL POOL**

505 N Michigan
Avenue
Magnificent Mile ①
+1 312 944 4100
*intercontinental
chicago.com*

No expense was spared in the design of
this Olympic-sized swimming pool – one
of the largest hotel pools in the country,
and Chicago's oldest. Constructed in
the art deco-era, it features beautifully
restored hand-painted Spanish tilework
and a lavish terra cotta fountain of
Neptune. Pool access is complimentary
with spa services, or you can purchase
a 25-dollar day pass.

448 PROMONTORY POINT

5491 S DuSable Lake
Shore Drive
Hyde Park ⑦
+1 312 742 5369
promontorypoint.org

There are two dozen beaches perfect for jumping into the lake on a hot day, but 'The Point' is a favorite thanks to its low-key profile and stunning skyline views. The spot was constructed in the 1930s with a small meadow designed by Alfred Caldwell, and is especially popular with a clan of open-water swimmers who take to the waters year-round.

449 LIGHTHOUSE BEACH

2601 Sheridan Road
Evanston
+1 847 328 6961
grosspointlighthouse.net

A train ride to the city's nearest suburb is worth it for a day at this idyllic swimming spot. Tucked into a small inlet, the modest beach is covered in soft white sand, and its protected exposure makes for mild waves. On shore, the 1873 Grosse Point Lighthouse makes a picturesque backdrop. There's a nominal beach fee for visitors.

450 BERGER PARK

6205 N Sheridan
Road
Edgewater ⑥
+1 773 761 0376
chicagoparkdistrict.com

On the north end of this modest park, a tiny breakwater of rocks protects a wading area whose color mimics the Caribbean Sea. The slip of a beach at the end of Rosemont Avenue is accessible only to residents, but park benches offer infinite sightlines, and a sweet little cafe with snacks and drinks.

5 DAY SPAS

451 AIRE ANCIENT BATHS

800 W Superior St
River West ①
+1 312 312 9610
beaire.com/aire-
ancient-baths-chicago

One of a handful of industrially designed public baths under the Aire family, Chicago's outpost is in a warehouse building dating to 1902. After changing into robes and wet shoes, guests are led into a candle-lit subterranean network of pools ranging in temperature, as well as a duo of steam rooms and plunge pools.

452 KING SPA

809 Civic Center
Drive
Niles ⑥
+1 847 972 2540
kingspa.com

Though it's anything but glamorous, family-friendly King Spa in suburban Niles is an oasis of unique caliber. The large space features nine special rooms that are activated by mineral-charged stones, inviting guests to lay on tatami mats or sit criss-cross to soak in the experience. Don't miss the food court, serving authentic Korean cuisine.

453 KOHLER WATERS SPA

2358 N Lincoln
Avenue
Lincoln Park ⑤
+1 312 245 9129
kohlerwatersspa
lincolnpark.com

An urban outpost of the famous rural Wisconsin spa destination, this location features some 50 hydrotherapy treatment services ranging from relaxing, essential oil–infused baths to invigorating hot and cold water therapies. Relaxation and plunge pools, sauna and steam room complete the Thermal Suite.

454 CHUAN SPA

AT: THE LANGHAM
330 N Wabash
Avenue
River North ①
+1 312 923 9988
chuanspa.com

This lofty five-star spa offers upscale services ranging from deep-cleansing facials to CBD-infused massages. But the real gem is its luxe locker room: after a dip in the pool and the hydro-vitality hot tub, work your way through a series of steam rooms, eucalyptus and salt-stone saunas, finishing off with a nap on a heated-stone lounger.

455 GALOS CAVES

6501 W Irving
Park Road
Portage Park ⑥
+1 773 283 7701
galoscaves.com

Crimean iodine salt from the Black Sea is the foundation for this unique spa experience. Modeled after the relaxing salt caves of Eastern Europe, Galos's pair of caves are covered in salt from floor to ceiling, sparsely decorated with soft lighting and simple lawn chairs. Guests sit in silence for 45 minutes soaking in the iodine salt's healing properties.

451 AIRE ANCIENT BATHS

5 scenic
BIKE RIDES

---

456 NORTH BRANCH TRAIL

Entrance at W Foster
Avenue, east of N
Cicero Avenue
North Park ⑥
+1 800 870 3666
fpdcc.com/places/
trails/north-branch-
trail-system/

For city cyclists interested in riding safely all the way to the suburban Chicago Botanic Garden, this paved 22-mile (32-kilometer) trail offers a rewarding 90-minute ride. It extends all the way south to the LaBagh Woods Forest Preserve, leading cyclists safely along the North Branch of the Chicago River cutting through woodlands and wetlands along the way.

457 BIG MARSH

11559 S Stony
Island Avenue
South Deering ⑧
+1 312 590 5993
bigmarsh.org

This impressive 300-acre bike park is a dream for leisurely rides and BMX action alike. A dirt singletrack trail features ladder bridges and gentle wooden rollers, and two professional asphalt pump tracks are suitable for all levels of ability. There are also three jump-line courses designed for a range of experience. Bike rental facility on site.

458 LAKEFRONT TRAIL

Entrances along the
trail from Ardmore
Avenue to 71st St
Various ②
chicagoparkdistrict.com

Lakefront cyclists have a dedicated lane
on this majestic trail that hugs the city's
lakeshore. Approximately 18.5 miles
(30 kilometers) of paved path are carved
through a half-dozen neighborhoods
on the North Side with plenty of scenic
spots to pause along the way. When the
weather's nice, this is one of the most
beautiful – and quickest – ways to travel
along the lake.

459 WICKER PARK

N Wicker Park
Avenue and
N Damen St
Wicker Park ④
+1 312 742 7553
chicagoparkdistrict.com

Though there are only a few dedicated
bike lanes carved into this charming
tree-lined neighborhood, there are plenty
of bike-friendly roads and quiet side
streets to string together a few hours-
long pleasure ride. Several exits from the
Bloomingdale Trail deposit bikers into
the heart of residential streets marked by
historic mansions, casual corner taverns
and hip eateries.

460 JACKSON PARK

6401 S Stony
Island Avenue
Jackson Park ⑦
+1 773 256 0903
chicagoparkdistrict.com

As one of the city's biggest, this park
is best experienced by bike due to its
diverse geographical makeup. Amassing
500 acres at the site of the Chicago
World's Fair of 1893, it's laid out on the
lake next to a series of water features that
foster a scenic range of flora and fauna.
Follow the bridge to Wooded Island at
the park's center.

CHICAGO FIRE ACADEMY

40 RANDOM FACTS & URBAN MYTHS

5 famous
MOVIE LOCATIONS

461 THE STAIRS AT UNION STATION FROM *THE UNTOUCHABLES*

225 S Canal St
West Loop Gate ④
chicagounion
station.com

Anyone who's seen this 1987 crime thriller knows the scene when a fictionalized Elliot Ness faces a shootout in Chicago's Union Station. The marble stairs, which connect the 1925 building's grand hall to its south entrance, were so worn with nearly a century of foot traffic that they were replaced in 2016 – fortunately retaining the classic deco-era character memorialized in the film.

462 CAMERON'S HOUSE FROM *FERRIS BUELLER'S DAY OFF*

370 Beech St
Highland Park

Filmed as a love letter to Chicago, the 1980s classic is full of cameos from the Art Institute to Wrigley Field. But perhaps the most iconic is the modernist glass house of Ferris's BFF, Cameron. Nestled in a wooded lot in suburban Highland Park, the private residence is an apt tribute to famed Chicago architect Mies van der Rohe.

461 THE STAIRS AT UNION STATION FROM *THE UNTOUCHABLES*

463 *HOME ALONE* HOUSE

671 Lincoln Avenue
Winnetka

True to the iconic Christmas film, this private residence is roomy enough to house a family as large as Kevin's. The 1920s, Georgian-style home has ten bedrooms and six bathrooms, and its sprawling yard still sports the iron-rod fence that it did in the 1990 film. In fact, it's become so famous, there's a Lego replica set.

464 THE BAR FROM *HIGH FIDELITY*

1150 N Damen
Avenue
Ukrainian Village ④
+1 773 489 5999

Championship Vinyl, the 2000 film's famed record shop, was just a set. But one of the best scenes between stars John Cusack and Lisa Bonet can be re-lived at The Rainbo Club, a dark and beloved hipster bar. Order a High Life, sink down into the red leather couch by the pinball machine, and watch the scenes play out in real time.

465 CITY HALL FROM *THE BLUES BROTHERS* SCENES

121 N LaSalle St
The Loop ②
+1 312 744 5000
chicago.gov

The hilarious final scene of this campy 1980 cult classic was filmed at the city's true City Hall: a classical revival-styled structure erected in 1905. Built over an entire city block, the building features four nearly identical entrances and foyers, and houses offices for the mayor and several city and county departments.

5 HISTORIC LANDMARKS

466 FORT DEARBORN SITE

SW corner E Wacker
Drive at N Michigan
Avenue
The Loop ②
chicago.gov

Erected in 1803 on the south bank of what is now known as the Chicago River, this early American fort was at the time the westernmost point of the newly minted nation. Sunk into the cement of the modern sidewalks in the adjacent blocks, bronze markers outline the former walls of the fort.

467 COUCH TOMB

2045 N Lincoln
Park West
Lincoln Park ⑤
+1 312 642 4600
chicagohistory.org/
history-trail

Before Lincoln Park was Lincoln Park, its verdant greenspace held the City Cemetery: the final resting place of some 35.000 Chicagoans. When it was converted to public land in 1869, families were responsible for moving their dead to alternative cemeteries. Most complied; others simply left them behind. Couch Tomb, for reasons unknown, was the sole structure left standing.

468 STATUE OF THE REPUBLIC

6401 S Stony
Island Avenue
Hyde Park ⑦
chicago.gov

Despite the massive impact the Chicago World's Fair of 1893 had on the city's history, there's little physical evidence. That's because the fair's exhibition buildings were designed to be temporary and destroyed. One lovely homage is this gilded bronze statue: a miniature (though still large) version of the original, completed in 1918 to commemorate the fair's 25th anniversary.

469 UNION STOCKYARD GATE

W Exchange Avenue
at S Peoria St
Canaryville ⑦

Carl Sandburg's famous 1914 poem, *Chicago*, lent the city some of its most lasting nicknames, including "Hog Butcher for the World." It was here, at the Union Stock Yards, that Chicago surpassed the rest of the country in meatpacking. The grandeur of the gate's design alluded to the enormous impact of the industry on the locals.

470 HAYMARKET MEMORIAL

175 N Desplaines St
West Loop Gate ④
chicago.gov

The evening of May 4, 1886, began as a peaceful rally in support of the recently proposed eight-hour workday. But a bomb thrown into the crowd triggered multiple deaths, injuries, trials, and a permanent shift in the perception of labor disputes across the country. This memorial and plaque mark the spot.

5 INFAMOUS LOCATIONS

471 BIOGRAPH THEATER ALLEY

2433 N Lincoln
Avenue, alley
Lincoln Park ⑤
+1 773 871 3000
victorygardens.org

In July 1934, a sting was arranged to apprehend mobster John Dillinger, aka 'public enemy no. 1', at the Biograph Theater after catching a movie with a date. As Dillinger exited the theater, agents spotted him and called out to put his hands up. When he reached for a gun and tried to flee toward the alley, he was shot dead.

472 START OF THE GREAT CHICAGO FIRE

558 W De Koven St
Near South Side ④

The Great Chicago Fire of 1871 allegedly started in a barn located at this site. Of course, the barn has long since burnt down. Today, the infamous site is marked by two things: a commemorative bronze sculpture titled *Tongues of Flame*, by artist Egan Weiner, and the Chicago Fire Academy building.

473 **SITE OF THE EASTLAND DISASTER**

Clark Street Bridge and Wacker Drive
Riverwalk (2)
+1 224 764 2384
eastlanddisaster.org

In July 1915, while docked at Clark Street Bridge on the river to embark a few thousand working class passengers and their families for a pleasure cruise, the S.S. Eastland capsized and killed nearly 850 people, marking one of the nation's deadliest maritime disasters. A plaque at Wacker Drive and LaSalle streets marks the spot.

474 **SITE OF THE ST. VALENTINE'S DAY MASSACRE**

2122 N Clark St
Lincoln Park (5)

On Valentine's Day morning of 1929, seven men were lined up against a garage wall at this address and shot to death as part of a scheme for rival North Side gangs to control the area's organized crime. The garage wall was demolished in the 1960s, and a crime fanatic purchased the soiled bricks with plans for a mobster museum that never came to light.

475 **AL CAPONE'S FORMER HANGOUT**

2222 S Wabash Avenue
Motor Row District (3)

The Four Deuces bar and brothel, named after its address, used to occupy this spot on a stretch of the city's former vice district. For a handful of years in the early 1920s, it was home to the Chicago Outfit: the gang with which an up-and-coming young bootlegger named Al Capone was learning the ropes. The building was razed in 1963.

5 *facts about*

CHICAGO HOT DOGS

476 BEEF OR BUST

Hot dogs were first introduced to Chicagoans by Viennese brothers-in-law Samuel Landany and Emil Reichel at the Chicago World's Fair of 1893. Their popularity funded a brick-and-mortar store: the Vienna Sausage Co. As practicing Jews, the brothers-in-law did not consume pork, nor incorporate it into their sausages. To this day, authentic Chicago hot dogs are all-beef.

477 "DRAGGED THROUGH THE GARDEN"

Commonly associated with Chicago-style hot dogs, this phrase typically graces the menu – or lips – of vendors serving more than one style, to differentiate. The 'garden' refers to the assortment of fresh ingredients affiliated with a quintessential Chicago dog. Most locals won't have it any other way.

478 SEVEN INGREDIENTS

Chicago-style hot dogs are loaded with seven specific condiments and ingredients, and die-hard dog fans layer them in a specific order. Starting with a steamed poppy seed bun and the pure-beef dog itself, add 1) a squirt of yellow mustard; 2) a layer of neon-green pickle relish; 3) a scoop of finely diced white onions; 4) a couple of juicy red tomato slices tucked inside the top half of the bun; 5) a pickle spear layered parallel with the hot dog, usually facing down; then 6) two inch-long sport peppers laid on top; and finally 7) a generous shake of celery salt.

479 "HOLD THE KETCHUP"

Authentic Chicago hot dogs are never, ever served with ketchup. In fact, asking for it will earn you some seriously dirty looks. But why? Because ketchup is made with sugar, it's reputed to throw off the natural acidic balance combined by a Chicago-style hot dog's symphony of flavors.

480 POPPY SEED BUN

Another Jewish-rooted influence, poppy seed buns demarcate authenticity in a Chicago-style hot dog. Their origin traces back to the early 1900s, when eastern European immigrants were introducing traditional bread recipes to Chicago patrons. Rosen's, one of the earliest bakeries to open after the Chicago World's Fair, remains a go-to for authentic poppy seed buns.

5 elements of the
CHICAGO FLAG

481 RED STARS

Designed in 1917 by Wallace Rice, Chicago's flag had just two stars, representing the two most significant events in the city's history: the Great Chicago Fire of 1871, and the Chicago World's Fair of 1893. A third star was added in 1933 to honor the Century of Progress Exhibition; a fourth was added in 1939 to commemorate Fort Dearborn.

482 WHITE BARS

The three white bars of the Chicago flag represent the three areas of the city: the North Side, the West Side, and the South Side. There is no East Side to Chicago – that's where Lake Michigan lies.

483 BLUE BARS

The two sky blue bars represent not two, but four bodies of water significant to the city. The top represents Lake Michigan and the North Branch of the Chicago River, while the bottom represents the Great Canal and the South Branch of the river.

484 SIX-POINTED STARS

When Rice designed the flag, six-pointed flags were an anomaly: as a scholar of flags, he'd never seen one on another flag, and described it as "singularly a Chicago star." Besides, at that time, five-pointed stars largely represented sovereign states – unfitting for a city flag. Each of the stars' six points has its own individual meaning, too.

485 FUTURE STARS

A fifth star has been proposed numerous times for various events: in the 1980s, in honor of Harold Washington, the city's first Black mayor; in the 1990s to commemorate a particularly devastating flood; to represent the Special Olympics, which were founded in Chicago.

5 local
LEGENDS and LORE

486 THE CURSE OF THE BILLY GOAT AND THE CHICAGO CUBS

William "Billy Goat" Sianis, a Cubs fan, had purchased two tickets to the 1945 World Series at Wrigley Field: one for him, and one for his goat, Murphy. When the goat was denied entrance to the ballpark, the enraged Sianis announced to then owner P.K. Wrigley, "The Cubs ain't gonna win no more. The Cubs will never win a World Series so long as the goat is not allowed in Wrigley Field." Despite numerous attempts to break the curse by introducing subsequent goats into Wrigley Field, it was 71 years before the Cubs won the World Series again.

487 WINDY CITY ORIGINS STORY

Yes, it's windy in Chicago. But the Windy City got its nickname not from its billowy disposition on Lake Michigan, but from the bellows of politicians that claimed it as their own in the late 1800s. As an epicenter of economy and politics, Chicago and its rising class were often seen by rival states as single-minded, seemingly blowing a whole lot of hot air at the competition.

488 **"THE ONION"**

Nicknames like "The City of Big Shoulders" and "The City that Works" are commonplace now, but Chicago was originally called "The Onion." The word *Chicago* is a butchered French interpretation of *shikaakwa*, a Native American word for the *Allium tricoccum* plant, otherwise known as wild garlic. The first known reference to the area described as "Checagou" was in the late 17th century by a French explorer, noting in his journal the prevalence of wild garlic. To this day, wild allium sometimes grows in patches along unkempt swaths of the city.

489 **CHOCOLATE AROMA IN THE WEST LOOP**

Visitors to the West Loop sometimes detect a wafting scent of chocolate. That's because the Blommer Chocolate Factory, the largest chocolate-ingredient supplier in the country, is located on Kinzie and Desplaines in one of the most pedestrian-dense neighborhoods in the city. Though one local fan's "Daily Chicago Chocolate Smell Map" is no longer updated with forecasts, your nose knows.

490 **"CITY IN A GARDEN"**

Urbs in Horto, or "City in a Garden," is the city's official motto, adopted in 1837 when it was incorporated. At the time, it hardly resembled an oasis in nature. But by the time architect Daniel Burnham was charged with drawing a city plan in the early 1900s, the goal was for every citizen to be within walking distance of a park.

5 myths about the
GREAT CHICAGO FIRE
of 1871

491 IT WAS STARTED BY A COW

The most popular belief about the fire's origins is that it was started in the small barn of the O'Leary residence, near 558 W DeKoven Street, when the family cow kicked over a lantern. Neighboring the barn was the first structure to be consumed by the fire: a wooden shed. Despite the rumours, the O'Learys were never officially held blame, and were exonerated 125 years later. (The cow was, too.)

492 THE WHOLE CITY BURNED DOWN

Due to strong winds from the southwest, the fire burned north and east of its origin in the O'Leary's barn, hopping the Chicago River not once, but twice, eating up the downtown area's dense network of wooden sidewalks and roads. Aided by a light rain, the fire burnt itself out within 48 hours, leaving the western and southern portions of the city virtually untouched. In all, the fire burned a little over three square miles of the city – about a third of its area.

493 THE CHICAGO WATER TOWER WAS THE ONLY SURVIVING STRUCTURE

Because it was one of the very few buildings in the heart of the city to stand, the 55-meter-tall water tower became a symbol of recovery and resilience. The entire surrounding downtown was singed to the ground, but several other random structures dodged the flames.

494 IT WAS THE DEADLIEST FIRE IN AMERICAN HISTORY

The deadliest fire in American history did, in fact, happen on October 8, 1871, but not in Chicago. It was 250 miles to the north, in Peshtigo, Wisconsin. The Great Chicago Fire killed about 300 people and destroyed approximately 3.3 square miles, while the Peshtigo Fire killed between 1200 and 2500 and destroyed 1,5 million acres. Thirty years later, another deadly fire would mar the city's history: the Iroquois Theater Fire of 1903, which resulted in more than 600 deaths.

495 IT TOOK MANY YEARS FOR THE CITY TO RECOVER

In reality, rebuilding began as soon as the smoulder died down, and the progress was swift. In the early 1870s, Chicago was the epicenter of the country's lumber industry as well as the center of railroad and trade, so funneling in supplies and labor was easy. Neighboring cities sent immediate relief, and there was an outpouring of aid from international allies. The response was so fast that within just a few years, the city was completely rebuilt by the time it opened for the Chicago's World's Fair in 1893.

5 *Chicago* TRADITIONS

496 **DIBS**

Anyone who's ever had to dig out a car from under a foot of snow knows how laborious the task can be. Chicagoans have a system of marking shoveled territory to save their backs. Locals call "dibs" by placing a personal item in their spot. Typically, it's a lawn chair or an empty bucket, but some get more creative. The tradition has been in place since the especially brutal Blizzard of '67, when a record 36 inches of snow – enough for an entire winter – fell in a little over a week's time.

497 **SLASHIES**

In New England, liquor stores are called package stores or "packys;" in Michigan, they're party stores. And in Chicago, if there's a bar in the back, they're slashies: bar/liquor stores that both sell packaged liquor and offer drinks on premise. Due to a local law established long ago, Chicago taverns are allowed to sell a percentage of goods to-go. Patrons can pick up a six-pack to go, and have a quick shot of malört before they do.

498 MALÖRT

The city's rich Swedish history led to the popularity of this traditional digestif. During the Prohibition era, a local distiller by the name of Carl Jeppson began peddling his brand of malört: a bitter wormwood-based liquor. The flavor of Jeppson's Malört is so pungent, it eventually earned a reputation as a shot you'd only take on a dare. With the 21st-century cocktail renaissance came modern interpretations – notably, a palpable version produced by local Letherbee Distillers called, simply, Bësk.

499 DYING THE RIVER GREEN

Every St. Patrick's Day, the Chicago Plumbers Union dyes the Chicago River a shockingly bright green, inspired by the 'Emerald Isle' of Ireland. With a great deal of pomp and circumstance, locals line the river to watch as two large boats dispense dozens of gallons of vegetable-based dye, followed by a small fleet of speed boats to mix in the color.

500 SANTA ON THE EL

Every holiday season, St. Nicholas joins throngs of commuters to make his way through the city's public transportation system via the CTA Holiday Train, which appears for a few runs a day on each of the train lines. Santa himself rides on a special open-air car with enough room for his sleigh, and the adjoining cars are kitted out with festive lights and holiday music, and lined in wrapping paper.

INDEX

COLOPHON

EDITING *and* COMPOSING — Lauren Viera

GRAPHIC DESIGN — Joke Gossé and doublebill.design

PHOTOGRAPHY — Giovanni Simeone

COVER IMAGE — Street art by Cody Hudson (secret 346)

The addresses in this book have been selected after thorough independent research by the author, in collaboration with Luster Publishing. The selection is solely based on personal evaluation of the business by the author. Nothing in this book was published in exchange for payment or benefits of any kind.

The author and the publisher have made every effort to obtain permission for all illustrations and to list all copyright holders. Interested parties are requested to contact the publisher.

D/2022/12.005/20

ISBN 978 94 6058 3483

NUR 510, 513

© 2023 Luster Publishing, Antwerp

First reprint, December 2023

lusterpublishing.com — THE500HIDDENSECRETS.COM

info@lusterpublishing.com

Printed in Italy by Printer Trento.